BUTTERCREAM
ONE-TIER WONDERS

Valeri Valeriano & Christina Ong

D&C
David and Charles

www.stitchcraftcreate.co.uk

CONTENTS

CLASSIC

ARTISTIC

MONOCHROMATIC

SCENIC

ROMANTIC

RUSTIC

SHABBY CHIC

GEOMETRIC

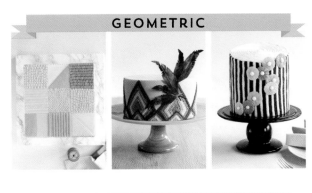

METALLIC

ECCENTRIC

INTRODUCTION

Back in 2011 when we discovered that butter and icing sugar are not just for spreading on toast and sprinkling on pancakes, we were amazed at the wonders a combination of these two humble ingredients can create. We were instantly obsessed!

We were very certain that we wanted to become cupcake pros and therefore we named ourselves 'Queen of Hearts Specialty Cupcakes, Edible Bouquets and More'. (It is the longest company name you could ever imagine, isn't it?). The 'More' referred to the fact that we would make cookies, pies and other small treats, but never really thought of making towering multi-tiered cakes, because we thought anything bigger than a cupcake was just too scary and too stressful.

Then one day a friend called us and ordered a birthday cake for herself and, of course, we couldn't say no. We thought that if it didn't turn out right, she would forgive us because we were friends. And so we did it.

We made her an eight-inch square cake (why did we start with square when we could have begun with an easier round cake, right?), with a simple graffiti decoration. She came back to us full of praises... *but*, with a smiling face, she started to tell us how the celebration went and how, as she was about to blow out the candles, the back part of the cake had fallen off. The frosting CAME OFF! But because she was a friend (thank goodness), she was fine about it and just thought it was funny!

This episode might have confirmed our fear of making any cake bigger than a cupcake, but after hearing her story, instead of being discouraged, we were determined to figure out what went wrong, and make sure it that it didn't happen again. So if you guessed that we did not crumb coat our cake properly, you were right! We didnt even know what crumb coating was! We had just covered the cake with a thick layer of buttercream and decorated straight onto that. Technically, buttercream is heavy and it will not stick to the cake properly unless it's been crumb coated. What happened to us, could happen to you too – but we'd like to help you avoid the mistakes that we made.

That is basically our inspiration for this book. Whenever we look back at our cake-y journey, we can't help but laugh about it. So we thought, we'd make a book that is all about single-tier cakes: starting from the basics, to simple carving and building up to dowelling taller cakes, in addition to giving you over thirty ideas on how to decorate your cake in ten different styles. You may think that it is 'easier' to decorate single-tier cakes but, in fact, there is always a danger of over-decorating, because you wanted to put all your ideas on such a small canvas.

In this book, we don't just help you build up your skills, but we also divide the cake styles into different themes: Shabby Chic, Romantic, Rustic to name just a few. After trying to re-create the projects in the book, please do explore how to mix and match the techniques to come up with your own unique designs. Also try changing the colour palette, for example, if you change the Black & White Pinstripe cake to pastel rainbow stripes or use gradient colours, it could become a soft romantic or a shabby chic-themed cake.

There is more to it than just following our cake projects and so we truly hope that you will want to innovate and develop your own styles too. And when you do, please share them with us because we would love to see them! We hope you enjoy this book.

Happy BUTTERCREAM cake decorating!

Valerie   Christine

BUTTERCREAM BASICS

Basic buttercream recipe

With this recipe, the one thing you should remember is never over-beat your buttercream. If you do it will become grainy and the edges are likely to 'break' when you pipe your flowers, borders and textures. When you over-beat, you incorporate lots of air in your buttercream, thus, the surface will have holes or 'air-pockets' when you spread it on the cake, making it hard to smooth. This is a 'crusting' buttercream that we developed to suit all climates.

A hand-held mixer is not usually as powerful as a stand mixer, so if you are using a hand-held one, make sure you fold your mixture manually first until the ingredients are incorporated. This helps to avoid over-beating as well.

What is so good about our recipe is that a little less or more of a certain ingredient is fine. So if your buttercream is too stiff, add water or milk. If it is too thin, just add icing (confectioners') sugar. Adjust it as you need to – all in moderation of course. You may use your buttercream straight away to cover and decorate your cakes but if you think it is too soft, we suggest you chill it in the fridge for about an hour, or touch the surface – if it is hard enough, you may take it out of the fridge. DO NOT add more icing sugar just to make it stiff.

TIP

Keep your buttercream in the refrigerator and store it in an air-tight container or food storage bags. You can freeze it for up to a month, letting it defrost thoroughly at room temperature before use. Do not beat it again in a mixer, just mix it manually. But of course, nothing is better than lovely fresh buttercream!

You will need

- 227g (8oz) butter, room temperature
- 113g (4oz) medium soft vegetable fat (shortening) (Trex), at room temperature, OR 227g (8oz) of soft spreadable vegetable fat (shortening) (Crisco)
- 2–3 tsp vanilla essence, or your choice of flavouring
- 1 tbsp water or milk (omit if you live in a hot country or whenever the temperature is hot)

- 600g (1lb 5oz) icing (confectioners') sugar, sifted, if you are using medium soft vegetable fat (shortening) OR 750g (1lb 10oz) icing sugar, sifted, if you are using soft spreadable vegetable fat (shortening)
- Mixer (hand-held or stand mixer)
- Mixing bowls
- Spatula
- Sieve (sifter/strainer)
- Measuring spoons

1. Beat the butter at medium speed until soft and pale (about one to two minutes). Some brands of butter are more yellow in colour, so to make it paler you can increase the beating time to about two to five minutes.

2. Add the vegetable fat (shortening) and beat for another 20 to 30 seconds or less. Make sure that it is well incorporated and that there are no lumps.

Important note: As soon as you add anything to the butter, you must limit your beating time to 20–30 seconds or even less.

3. Add vanilla essence, or your flavour of choice and water, or milk, then beat at medium speed for about 10 to 20 seconds until well incorporated.

4. Slowly add the sifted icing (confectioners') sugar and beat at medium speed for another 20 to 30 seconds or until everything is combined. You may want to fold the ingredients together manually before beating to avoid puffing clouds of sugar round your kitchen. Make sure you scrape the sides and bottom of your bowl, as well as the blade of your mixer, so you don't miss any lumps of icing sugar.

5. Lastly, after scraping the bowl, beat again for about 20 to 30 seconds and do not over-mix. This yields a perfect piping consistency of buttercream.

TIP

You may add milk but if you do you can only keep your buttercream for two to four days, as milk has a shorter shelf-life. If you use water, you will be able to keep it for longer — about five to ten days. If you find the vegetable shortening does not incorporate well enough to the butter and you see lumps or you think that it is a really hard consistency, in future, beat the vegetable shortening separately first and then proceed as normal.

Coverage

If you make the basic buttercream recipe with the amounts given, one batch will yield approximately 1–1.1kg (2lb 7^1/$_2$oz) of buttercream. This will be enough to cover the top, the sides and fill a 20cm (8in) round or square cake depending on the design. This can be your guide to determine how much frosting you need to prepare. If you have any left over, just label it with the date you made it and store it in the fridge.

About vegetable fat, aka shortening

This is a white solid fat made from vegetable oils, and is usually flavourless or at least bland. You can find it in most supermarkets, next to the butter and margarines. It plays a very important role in our recipe as it helps make our buttercream stable, so you do not need to add too much icing sugar to make a stiff consistency, thus your frosting will have just the right sweetness. It also allows the surface of the decorated cake to 'crust' so it is not too sticky.

Different brands of vegetable fat (shortening) have different consistencies. If the consistency of your shortening is hard, defrost it in the microwave first to soften and use 113g (4oz). If it is somewhat medium-soft to slightly hard, like Trex, use 113g (4oz) as well. If it is soft and very spreadable, like Crisco, you will have to double the amount to 227g (8oz).

Colouring

Colours bring your cake to life, can set a mood, attract attention, or make a statement. Hence, it is important to choose and prepare your tinted buttercream properly. Since this book is all about different themes, it is best to research the perfect colour palette to be able to get the appropriate colours to use per project.

We have highlighted the things you should remember when mixing colours.

- Make sure that your buttercream is at room temperature when tinting, so that the colours blend together.
- Add paste colours a little at a time using a clean cocktail stick (toothpick), and never re-use it as it will contaminate the paste. Or tint a small amount of buttercream to create a strong colour, then use that to add to your bigger batch of buttercream so that you can control the strength of colour gradually.
- When tinting buttercream, mix it manually. *Do not* put it into the mixer to blend it even if it is a huge amount because there is a tendency that you will over-beat it.
- Bear in mind that it is normal for buttercream to deepen in colour after a short while, especially with darker colours. Prepare at least two or three hours ahead of time to allow for colour change.
- Prepare more than enough tinted buttercream for big projects. You don't want a part of your cake to be a different colour, do you?

- To lighten the colour add more untinted buttercream, to darken the colour, add more colouring.
- If your buttercream is a little yellowish, you can make it whiter by adding a hint of violet or a whitener, such as Sugarflair Super White. If you are aiming for a light shade, whiten the buttercream first then add the desired colour.
- If the colours that you have made are very bright, you can tone them down by adding a hint of black, brown or violet.
- Food colouring comes as powder, gel or pastes. *Do not* use powder food colour to tint your buttercream directly as it will not dissolve properly. When mixed, it will look as if it is well blended but after a while, the tiny granules will start to dissolve and will show speckles of colours. If this is your only option, we suggest that you dissolve the powder in a very small drop of water, bearing in mind that the more liquid you put in buttercream, the softer it becomes.
- If you are using a liquid food colouring like those in squeeze bottles, it is sometimes hard to control the amount that comes out, especially if you need even less than a drop. You can tint a small amount of buttercream then use that to add colour to your bigger batch, rather than putting colours directly to your buttercream.
- Food colouring pastes and gels come in many different brands and each has a different concentration and yields a different shade. Whatever brand you have locally, you should always try it first in a small batch so as to prevent wasting the buttercream.

Using props

Because the cakes in this book are single-tier ones they can be quite small, and therefore you do not need to surround them with an elaborate range of props. You can enhance your cake display with the simplest things that you can find at home or even in your garden. For example, you could place a single hibiscus flower beside the cake or scatter a few around it. If you can't find a real one, you could make a paper flower.

Alternatively, try wrapping a strip of burlap lace around an empty tin and add your birthday message onto it for a shabby chic theme. Then present the tin together with the cake. We could go on and on about ideas, but what we are simply trying to emphasize here is that adding some props when you set up your cake will show it at its very best.

Styling your cake board

Besides propping, another way to add glamour to your cake is by dressing up your cake boards. This is a blind spot for some, and so often people leave their boards uncovered. Even if your cake is good, if it's poorly presented it may disappoint. Therefore, take it from us, say 'NO' to naked cake boards!

You will see from the projects in this book that we have covered our boards with vinyl sticker paper (a 5m/5$^{1}/_{2}$yd roll costs very little and can cover about eight or more 25cm/10in boards), gift wrap, scrapbooking papers, fabrics etc. You can even write a letter or lyrics of your favourite song on a large piece of paper and use that to cover your board. We have also used slate boards, chopping boards and placemats (board and glass types) to replace the usual boards. There are so many inexpensive things that you can use or even create yourself, but balance the cake design with the board and, unless your cake is very plain, don't make everything too elaborate.

9

Equipment

Measuring cups and spoons

Cocktail sticks

Disposable piping (pastry) bags

Sieve (sifter/strainer)

Cake turntable

Paint palette

Paint brushes

Cookie cutters

Stencils

Greaseproof (wax) paper

Palette knives

Food colouring pastes/gels

Ruler

Set square/protractor

Spatulas

Flower nail

Nozzles

Palette knife painting set

Cake boards/drums

Tweezers

Cake leveller

Cake scraper

Non-woven cloth

Pen/pencil

Small kitchen knife

Spoons

Couplers

Stand mixer

Scissors

Weighing scales

Hand mixer

Mixing bowls

Cake recipes

Madeira cake

This recipe makes a nice dense sponge cake that is easy to carve and stack – and it's absolutely delicious! The quantities given below will make a 20cm (8in) round cake.

You will need

- 250g (12oz) unsalted butter
- 250g (12oz) caster (superfine) sugar
- 250g (12oz) self-raising (-rising) flour
- 125g (6oz) plain (all-purpose) flour
- 5 large eggs
- ⅛tsp salt
- 2–3tbsp milk

1. Pre-heat the oven to 160°C or 325°F. Grease your cake tin, line the base with baking (parchment) paper and grease the paper.

2. Cream the butter and sugar in a large bowl until light, fluffy and pale. Sift the flours together in a separate bowl.

3. Beat in the eggs, one at a time, beating the mixture well between each one and adding a tablespoon of flour with the last egg to prevent the mixture curdling.

4. Gently fold in the flour and salt, with enough milk to give a mixture that falls slowly from the spoon.

5. Transfer to the lined cake tin and bake for an hour to an hour and a half. When the cake is ready it will be well risen, firm to the touch and a skewer inserted into the centre will come out clean.

6. Turn it out onto a wire rack to cool completely.

Chocolate mud cake

This recipe makes a dense cake that behaves well when you use it for stacking and carving.

You will need

- 250g (9oz) salted butter
- 250g (9oz) dark or milk chocolate (chopped or broken)
- 8tsp instant coffee
- 180ml (6¼fl oz) water
- 150g (5½oz) self-raising (-rising) flour
- 150g (5½oz) plain (all-purpose) flour
- 60g (2oz) cocoa powder (unsweetened is best)
- ½tsp bicarbonate of soda (baking soda)
- 500g (17oz) caster (superfine) sugar
- 5 eggs, lightly beaten
- 70g (2½oz) vegetable oil
- 125ml (4fl oz) buttermilk (to make: add one tablespoon lemon juice or white vinegar to one cup of milk and let it sit for 5–10 minutes)

1. Preheat your oven to 160°C or 320°F, then grease and line your baking tins.

2. Combine the butter, water and coffee in a saucepan over heat until they come to a slow boil. Turn off the heat and pour in the chocolate, stirring until it is completely melted. Set aside.

3. Sift the flours, cocoa powder, sugar and bicarbonate of soda (baking soda) together in a large bowl, and make a well in the centre.

4. Pour in the eggs, buttermilk, oil and chocolate mixture and stir vigorously with a wooden spoon until there are no lumps.

5. Pour into your prepared tins and bake for approx 45 minutes for a 15cm (6in) cake or an hour and 15 minutes for a 20cm (8in) cake. Remove the cake from the oven when a skewer inserted in the middle comes out clean.

6. Allow the cakes to cool completely in the tins before removing them.

TIP

These quantities will make a 23 x 7.5cm (9 x 3in) round cake, a 20 x 10cm (8 x 4in) round cake, a 15 x 10cm (6 x 4in) round cake and approx. eight cupcakes, or a 20 x 7.5cm (8 x 3in) square cake.

Stacking and Dowelling

As your cake becomes taller you must add some structure to support it, to make it sturdy so that it will not collapse. You will need plastic or wooden dowels (or even large plastic straws) inserted properly into the lower layers of the cake, to bear the weight of the cake above and to make sure that each layer does not get squashed and collapse.

You can stack as many as three cake sponges without needing to dowel but as soon as you need to increase the height with more cake sponges, make sure you support the structure with dowels.

You will need

- Four cake sponges of your chosen size
- Three 1–2mm (1/16in) thin cake boards (fairly sturdy but still possible to cut – not cake cards)
- Cake drum
- Cake leveller or serrated knife
- Plastic or wooden dowels
- Wire cutters or heavy-duty scissors
- Pencil or pen
- Glue

TIP

To cut dowels that are exactly the same height as the layer of cake to be dowelled, you can push a dowel right into it from the top until it touches the cake board, then mark the place on the dowel that the top surface of the cake reaches, using a pencil or a pen, then remove the dowel and cut it off at the marked length.

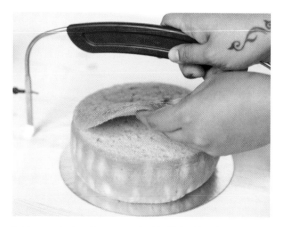

1. Use a cake leveller or serrated knife to trim the top surface of all the cake sponges to make them level.

2. Cut the thin boards about 5–10mm (1/4– 1/2in) bigger than the size of the cake or slightly bigger if you want the buttercream to be thicker. Usually you can use the bottom of the baking tin that you used to bake the cakes as your guide. Glue two thin boards together back to back (with the silver-coating outwards) and insert a dowel through the middle to create a hole. Keep turning the dowel around to make the hole slightly bigger so that it is easier to insert later.

3. Place the first two cake sponges on the third thin board, filling between them with buttercream. Measure and, using the wire cutters or heavy-duty scissors, cut dowels that are exactly the same height as the cake.

4. Insert the dowel rods into the bottom layer, evenly spaced about 4cm (1½in) in from the edge of the marked outline. Push the dowel rods straight down until each touches the cake board. The number of dowels to use depends on the size of the cake.

5. Apply a thin layer of buttercream on the top of the cake, just enough to cover the protruding dowels, then secure and stick the thin board to your cake drum using the glue. Do not just use buttercream or royal icing to stick the thin board to the drum as it could still slide about.

6. Repeat the process described in steps 3 and 4 to stack the other two cake sponges onto the glued-together thin boards, then position on top of the bottom two cakes.

7. Measure and cut a long dowel which is the height of the whole cake.

8. Insert the long dowel centrally right the way to the bottom of the cake.

Covering Cakes

The first step, before you can add any wonderful decoration, is to know how to cover the cake, making sure that the buttercream sticks to it and provides a clean base. You need to crumb coat, and then create a smooth surface. Further techniques for creating textured surfaces can be found within the cake projects.

Crumb Coating

Crumb coating means applying a thin layer of buttercream all over your cake to secure the loose crumbs. This is a very important step that you should not miss as this makes your outer layer of buttercream stick to the cake, giving the heavy piped and textured designs something to adhere to.

1. Use a round nozzle or just snip the end off a piping bag, then, using the same buttercream that will go on the rest of the cake, pipe around the cake with a good firm pressure so the buttercream sticks to the cake.

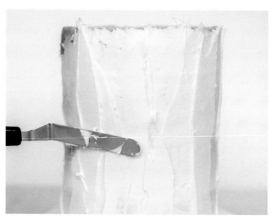

2. Use a palette knife to spread the buttercream all over the cake, applying even pressure and making sure to remove any excess buttercream with the edge of the palette knife.

3. You can use a cake scraper to even the thickness out or leave it as it is.

TIP

Chill the crumb coated cake in the fridge for about 20 to 30 minutes or until the surface is firm. It is better if you can place the cake in the freezer to speed up the process. If you don't chill the cake, it will be much more difficult to apply further decoration, such as a smooth layer of buttercream.

Smoothing

After the cake has been chilled for a while you can apply another layer of buttercream. The thickness of this layer will be a matter of taste. You can also use the thin board as your guide as to how thick your buttercream will be. For this stage you will need non-woven cloth, such as the interfacing used in sewing projects. This can be sourced online or from any reasonably large haberdashery.

1. Use a cake scraper to even out the thickness of buttercream all the way around the cake. Air-dry the cake at room temperature to allow it to crust for about 10 to 20 minutes.

2. When the cake is fully crusted (see tip below), place the non-woven cloth on the surface of the cake and rub gently with your fingers to smooth the surface. Repeat the same process all over the cake.

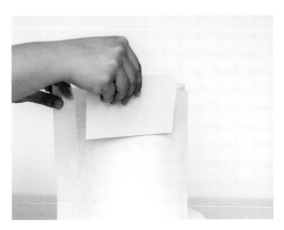

3. To make it perfectly smooth, place the non-woven cloth on the surface of the cake again and use the scraper, running it up and down over the cloth.

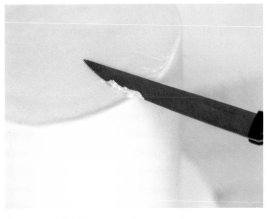

4. Use a small knife or the cake scraper to remove any excess buttercream on the edge of the cake.

TIP

Do not put it in the fridge or freezer again as the moist environment inside will prevent the buttercream from crusting. If the cake is dry and not tacky to touch, it means the cake is ready for smoothing.

Covering a sphere cake

Coating a sphere with buttercream presents its own particular problems. However, follow these steps to make an impressively smooth job of it.

1. Bake two half dome cakes using suitably shaped cake tins or heat-resistant bowls, such as Pyrex. Then level the cakes using a cake leveller or a serrated knife.

2. Cut off a small piece of cake at the top of one of the domes so it will sit steady on the board without rolling, then apply buttercream before sticking it to the board.

3. Fill the middle and place the other half of the cake on top of it to make a sphere. Use a short palette knife to spread out any excess buttercream.

4. Crumb coat the cake using the same buttercream that you will use for the top layer of cake covering.

5. Apply the thicker layer of buttercream and even out with a flexible Mylar scraper (or you can use any flexible plastic). Follow the curve of the cake then leave it to crust.

6. Dowel if the cake is large, then smooth the top coat with non-woven cloth, making sure that you follow the contours of the cake.

Piping textures

Some of the textures you will need to pipe to create the cakes in this book, are described within the projects themselves. However, where the method is a bit more involved or has cropped up several times, we have referred you to this section where we can explain the technique more thoroughly.

Borders

Shell border

Pipe a shell border by cutting a small hole at the tip of a piping bag or by using various nozzles. Hold the piping bag at a 30-degree angle with the tip of the nozzle touching the cake surface. Firmly squeeze the piping bag until the buttercream builds up and creates a small blob, then slightly lift the piping bag and pull down as you also gradually relax the pressure on the bag to create a pointed end of the shell. Start your next shell so that the wide end just covers the tail of the preceding shell to form a chain.

Ruffle borders

Using a small petal nozzle, such as Wilton 103 or 104, hold your piping bag at an angle with the cake surface, with the wide part of nozzle touching the surface of the cake. Continuously squeeze the piping bag with constant pressure and drag it along your border. Apply slight pressure to ensure that the ruffles stick to the cake. You can also slightly wiggle your piping bag to make wavy ruffles. Repeat the process for any succeeding ruffles making sure that they are close to each other and maintaining the angle. Variations can be 'back to back' (orange), 'upwards' (green), 'downwards' (yellow), wiggly etc.

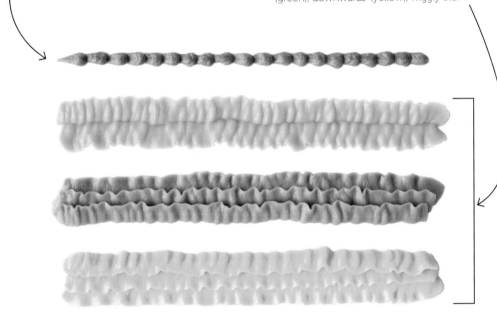

Loop border

The loop border that is used on our Vintage Birdcage and Steampunk Hat cakes is very simple to achieve. Fill a piping bag with your chosen colour and choose a suitable nozzle. Pipe with a tight circular motion, clockwise, making your circles tight so there are no gaps between the loops.

Bead border

Fill a piping bag with buttercream and use scissors to cut a tiny hole at the tip, or you can use a nozzle. Hold the piping bag straight on to the cake and gently squeeze the bag until a small dot appears. Make sure you stop squeezing the bag before you pull it away. Pipe dots in a neat row with each one touching its neighbour to create a border.

Piping flowers

Floral designs are amongst the most popular, and we often feature flowers, or whole bouquets on our cakes. The instructions for piping many flowers will be found within the cake projects, but if a flower appears often, we have referred you to this section to avoid repeating ourselves over and over again.

Sunflowers, waterlilies and simple leaves

A leaf nozzle will produce a perfect petal for a sunflower, if you follow the instructions below, but this technique can also be used to create waterlilies like those on our Impression of Waterlilies cake, the orange flowers on the Autumn Wreath, and to pipe simple leaves. All you need is to select the right nozzle and colour of buttercream.

1. Pipe a guide circle, then using a leaf nozzle such as Wilton 67 or 352 held at a 20 to 30 degree angle with one of the points touching your guide, squeeze the piping bag to create a wide base to the leaf. Pull slowly away, reducing the pressure on the bag until you reach the desired length, then stop squeezing and pull away abruptly.

2. Repeat the same process to pipe a layer of petals around the guide circle.

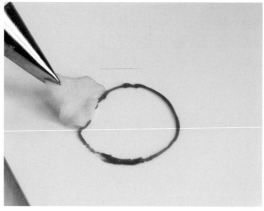

3. Pipe another layer of petals with a slightly steeper angle than the first, about 30 to 40 degrees, and make sure that they are close to the first layer of petals to avoid gaps.

4. Finally, using brown buttercream in a piping bag with a small hole at the tip, pipe little dots to create the centre of the flower.

Buds

Tiny buds can be added in sprays or singly to fill gaps in a design, or to add delicate features. We've used them in the Bas Relief and Country Window cakes.

To pipe a bud, take a small petal nozzle, such as Wilton 104, and hold your piping bag so the nozzle is flat on the cake surface with the wide end of the opening to the left. Gently squeeze the piping bag until it creates a half petal then pull the nozzle slightly to the right and upwards, then fold towards the centre. Pipe another petal over the first to overlap it, but this time work it in the opposite direction, so the wide part of the nozzle points right and you pull the petal left. Repeat until the bud is the size you require (in the case of small buds like those on the Country Window cake, this might only take two petals), then add a calyx using a piping bag with a small hole at the tip.

Simple petals

We use a wide variety of piping techniques to create flower petals, but here are two very simple ones. The first is used on the Lace Romance cake and the second for piping the frangipani on the Totally Tropical cake.

Lace Romance flowers

With two-tone buttercream (see the Lace Romance cake) in a bag with a Wilton 104 petal nozzle, position the nozzle at a 20 to 30 degree angle with the wide end of the opening touching the cake surface. The narrow end should be pointing outwards and in a 12 o'clock position. Give the piping bag a good squeeze without moving the nozzle at all. Stop when the petal is the right size. Repeat in curved overlapping rows, one below the other, reducing the number of petals in each row until the flower is complete.

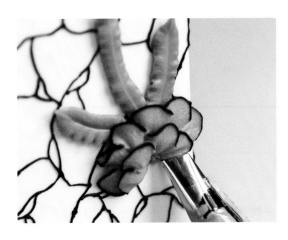

Frangipani

Using a Wilton 103 petal nozzle and two-tone yellow and white buttercream (see the Lace Romance cake for the two-tone effect) and holding the piping bag at a 20 to 30 degree angle with the yellow buttercream at the bottom, squeeze evenly and move the nozzle to the desired petal length. Make a tight turn to create a rounded tip, but do not make an arch. With the same pressure, pull the nozzle back to the base of the petal (a). Repeat and pipe four more petals all starting at the same central point (b).

a

b

Hibiscus and two-stroke leaves

The petals of the exotic hibiscus flowers on the Totally Tropical cake share the same piping technique with the leaves on the Sparkling Sensation cake. Use just steps 2 and 3 with green buttercream to achieve two-stroke leaves.

1. Pipe five guide marks radiating from a central point. Then start piping one side of the first petal by positioning your nozzle facing left, and positioned flat on the surface.

2. Squeeze the piping bag with constant, even pressure in a jiggling up and down motion until you reach the tip of your petal.

3. Turn the piping bag straight after piping the first side of the petal and continue piping the other side of the petal.

4. Repeat to pipe the other four petals.

5. For the flower centre, fill a piping bag with orange buttercream and cut a medium hole at the tip. Squeeze firmly and gradually pull upwards to create the central cone. Pipe yellow dots on the flower centre using a piping bag with a small hole cut at the tip.

Ruffle Flowers

These floral flourishes are perfect in so many designs – we find that we use them a lot! You can achieve a variety of effects with different nozzles but the basic technique is very simple. Here are some examples that you can try; we've shown them on a flower nail for clarity, but actually ruffle flowers should normally be piped directly onto the cake.

Ruffle one, Wilton 150

Ruffle two, Wilton 103

Ruffle three, Wilton 2D

Start from the outer edge for both ruffles one and two, hold the piping bag at a 20 to 30 degree angle and squeeze with even pressure, moving your hand up and down in a tight jiggling motion, while gradually moving clockwise (or counter-clockwise for left-handers). Repeat the same process for the succeeding layers.

Hold the piping bag with the nozzle flat to the surface of the cake. Squeeze with good pressure while slightly rotating left and right as you gradually pull the bag away.

Ruffle four, Wilton 104

Ruffle five, Wilton 103

Ruffle six, 97L

For both these ruffles, starting from the outer edge, hold a piping bag at a 20 to 30 degree angle and squeeze a simple petal (see Piping Flowers). Repeat to pipe petals in a circle until you finish the first layer. Pipe two or three more layers of petals. This ruffle makes the basic shape for a camellia.

Hold the piping bag with the nozzle in an upright position. Squeeze the bag as you drag the nozzle downwards and slightly wiggle it to create a wavy petal. Repeat to pipe more rows of petals.

Succulents

For the rose-like succulents for the Terrarium cake, pipe a blob of buttercream onto a flower nail to create a central mound. Onto this, pipe 'petals' like a rose (see Roses) starting at the centre and using a Wilton nozzle 150. Turn the flower nail and build up the layers until the succulent is the desired size. For the spikey succulent, pipe a cluster of fat spikes onto a flower nail with a Wilton open star nozzle 68. Pipe with even pressure then stop squeezing and pull the bag away. The succulents should be placed in the freezer until firm, usually about 10 to 20 minutes.

Roses

Surely the most popular of flowers, especially for enhancing a cake design, roses are easiest to create when piped onto a flower nail. We've used them extensively in this book, particularly on the Pail of Roses and Ball of Flowers cakes.

1. Position the Wilton 104 petal nozzle flat against the flower nail and squeeze the piping bag as you turn the nail to create a base.

2. Hold the nozzle vertically with the wide end touching the surface and slightly tilted inward, so that your central bud will have only a small opening. Squeeze the piping bag as you turn the nail until you make both ends meet.

3. While the nozzle is still slightly tilted inwards, turn the nail and pipe a curved petal in an arch-shape around the bud, slightly pushing the petal against the bud so there are no gaps. Each subsequent petal should begin slightly past the middle of the previous one and overlap it. Pipe about two to four short petals.

4. After creating the bud with few petals around it, hold the nozzle vertically and pipe four to five slightly longer and higher arched upright petals.

5. When piping the last few petals, tilt the nozzle slightly outwards and make the arches longer instead of higher. Pipe four to five outer petals.

6. Use scissors to lift the rose up from the flower nail. Gently slide the rose onto a board, ready to go into the freezer for 10 to 20 minutes.

Using wafer paper

Versatile wafer paper is perfect for creating large appliqués for decoration. It is stiff and very light, so it makes wonderful feathers, leaves and flowers that don't need to be supported by anything. And it can be painted so that you can give it any colour or pattern you desire.

You will need

- Wafer paper
- Florist wire, gauge 18–20, or any thin and bendable wire
- Scissors
- Clear alcohol such as vodka, or lemon extract

- Paint brush
- Paint palette
- Chosen food colouring pastes
- Small bowl with water
- Piping gel

1. Cut strips of wafer paper of the same width. The width will depend on your pattern. The feathers for the Steampunk Hat are about 4–5cm (1½–2in) wide. On one side of the wafer paper, apply a thin layer of piping gel then position the florist wire in the centre and stick another piece of wafer paper on top of it.

2. Ideally, leave to dry for several hours or overnight. Sketch your leaf or feather pattern, cut it out and transfer it to the wafer paper by tracing or drawing round it. Next cut around the pattern shape. Paint as desired. Make sure not to oversaturate the paint with lots of alcohol as it may cause the wafer paper to wrinkle.

Moulds

You can make a huge range of beautifully detailed shapes to add to your cakes using silicone moulds, which can be purchased in most specialist stores and online. We've made good use of them in our Eccentric cakes, the Steampunk Hat, Alice in Wonderland and Nicely Sliced cakes. To use the moulds press your chosen colour of buttercream in firmly with a palette knife to avoid any air bubbles. Freeze the mould for 10 to 20 minutes, then ease the shape out, touching it as little as possible with warm fingers, and apply it to your cake.

TIP

Do not freeze buttercream flowers or moulded shapes for too long, definitely not overnight, as condensation will form on the buttercream. This can make colours run and ruin your hard work. Freezing for 20 to 30 minutes, or until firm to the touch is enough.

BRODERIE ANGLAISE

The soft colours and delicate decoration of this cake evoke its lacy fabric inspiration. The eyelet design is created with small perforations shaped into simple flowers. These eyelet flowers perfectly compliment the ruffles and ribbons to produce a simple yet exquisite look.

You will need

- 20 x 20cm (8 x 8in) square cake, 13cm (5in) high
- 500g (1lb 2oz) white buttercream (Sugarflair Super White powder)
- 1–1.1kg (2lb 4oz–2lb 8oz) peach buttercream (Sugarflair Peach)
- 100–200g (3½–7oz) light peach buttercream (Sugarflair Peach)
- 100–200g (3½–7oz) grey buttercream (Sugarflair Liquorice)
- Baking (parchment) paper
- Scissors
- Ruler
- Pencil
- Cocktail stick (toothpick)
- Short angled palette knife
- Scraper
- Small piece of cardboard or plastic sheet
- Wilton ruffle nozzle 86
- Wilton writing nozzle no.1
- Wilton basketweave nozzle 47
- Wilton petal nozzle 150
- Piping bags
- Coupler
- Large pearl dragees (sugar balls)
- Tweezers
- Flower nail

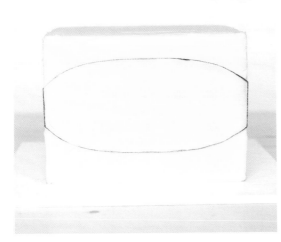

1. Stack and crumb coat your cake (see Buttercream Basics). Cut a piece of baking (parchment) paper measuring 5cm (2in) less than the height of the cake, and make the corners rounded as shown. Make four of these paper pieces and stick them on all sides of the cake, each 2.5cm (1in) from the top.

2. Apply peach buttercream all around the cake without covering the parchment paper. Then smooth the surface of the cake (see Buttercream Basics).

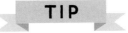

TIP

When covering the cake with two different colours, you will find it very helpful to cover one part with baking paper to prevent the colours mixing and to get precision in the shape of the design.

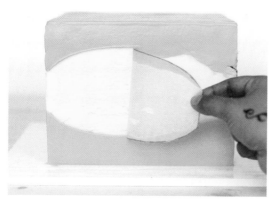

3. Use a cocktail stick (toothpick) to help you lift each piece of baking paper, then completely pull them off.

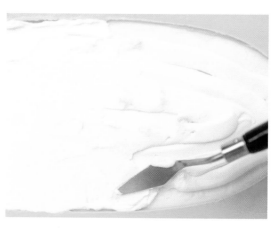

4. Use white buttercream to fill in the rounded panel on all sides. Make sure that it is the same thickness as the peach buttercream. Use a short angled palette knife to spread it carefully.

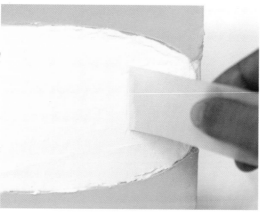

5. Use a small piece of cardboard or plastic sheet as a scraper to even out the buttercream, then smooth with a non-woven cloth after.

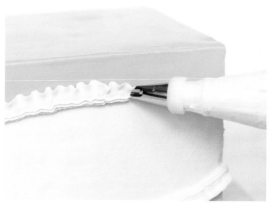

6. Use ruffle nozzle 86 and pipe a ruffle border around all the edges of the white central panel. Continuously squeeze the piping bag with the round part of the nozzle touching the edge of the central panel, and drag the piping bag following the shape.

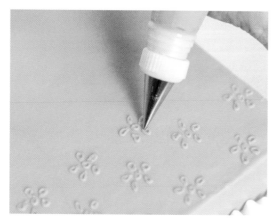

7. Using peach buttercream and the writing nozzle no.1, pipe a small five-petal flower with a tiny circle as the centre. Pipe staggered rows of the flowers all over the peach-coloured surfaces of the cake.

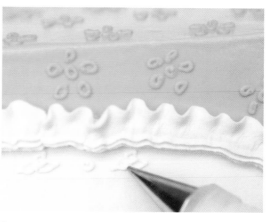

8. Around the edge of the white panel, pipe alternating three-petal flowers and small circles using white buttercream.

9. Wait about 30 minutes to an hour, until the buttercream surface is crusted well. Next cut off one end of the cocktail stick using scissors and use the blunt end to poke the floral details to exaggerate the holes.

10. Use the smooth side of the basketweave nozzle 47 to pipe short straight lines across the centre of the white panel using grey buttercream. Make sure you leave spaces in between these lines.

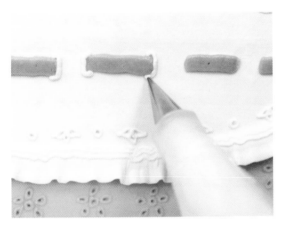

11. With writing nozzle no.1, pipe little 'brackets' on the ends of each of the grey 'ribbons' using white buttercream. Pipe a large ribbon bow in grey on each side of the cake. Finally add a few ribbon roses at the base (see the Ribbon Rose Heart cake for this technique) in light peach buttercream using the petal nozzle 150.

CHARMING CHALKBOARD

You can write any message you like on this distressed vintage chalkboard. It can easily be incorporated into the perfect theme to match your celebration, just by changing the floral accents and the words written on its invitingly smooth dark surface.

You will need

- 20cm (8in) round cake, 20cm (8in) high
- 1.2kg (2lb 10oz) black buttercream (Sugarflair Liquorice)
- 400–500g (14oz–1lb 2oz) white buttercream (Sugarflair Super White powder)
- 30–50g (1¼–1¾oz) light pink buttercream (Sugarflair Claret)
- 300–400g (10½–14oz) dusky pink buttercream (Sugarflair Dusky Pink)
- 300–400g (10½–14oz) violet buttercream (Sugarflair Grape Violet)
- 300–400g (10½–14oz) green buttercream (Sugarflair Gooseberry)
- 50–100g (1¾–3½oz) yellow buttercream (Sugarflair Autumn Leaf)

- Scraper
- Piping bags
- Palette knife
- Non-woven cloth
- Baking (parchment) paper
- Ruler
- Pencil
- Scissors
- Cocktail stick (toothpick)
- Wilton star nozzle 16
- Wilton chrysanthemum nozzle 81
- Wilton flower nozzle 14
- Wilton leaf nozzle 352
- Wilton petal nozzle 102

1. Stack and crumb coat your cake (see Buttercream Basics). Then make the chalkboard colour: blend the white buttercream by adding it gradually to a bowl containing the black buttercream. Start with 100g (3½oz) and add only as much as you need until the black becomes deep grey. Then apply it to the crumbcoated cake. You do not have to smooth it yet, just even it out with a scraper.

2. Use the remaining white buttercream to pipe small blobs randomly all over the cake. Make sure you leave spaces in between and do not overdo it. Use the tip of your palette knife to spread the buttercream using small round or back and forth movements.

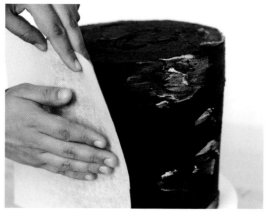

3. Use the non-woven cloth and lightly smooth the surface of the cake (see Buttercream Basics).

4. Draw an arch on a piece of baking (parchment) paper as a guide for where the top floral feature will go, and cut it out. Ours measured 20cm (8in) wide. Position it on the cake and use a cocktail stick (toothpick) to draw a guide mark, then remove. Repeat to create a guide for the lower floral feature, using the same paper guide flipped over.

5. Use white buttercream in a piping bag with a small hole at the tip, or use a Wilton writing nozzle no.1 or 2, to write anything you wish. For this cake we used the word 'Love'. Make sure that it is positioned centrally between your arched guide marks.

6. Add some white scribbles, scrolls, hearts, dots, or leaves, to decorate your cake, but don't go above the top arched guide mark or below the bottom one.

TIP

7. Using the dusky pink and star nozzle 16, pipe a very small swirl on the guide mark. Pipe more along the mark, leaving gaps for other flowers. Do this on both the arches.

If you accidentally made a mistake, just use the palette knife and blend the white buttercream into the black background. If you make a lot of mistakes and the background becomes too light, just add a thin layer of black buttercream on top and repeat the process. Since the background is black, once you have covered the cake, leave it to crust for three to four hours so that the black doesn't bleed into the white writing and decoration.

8. Pipe small chrysanthemum flowers using chrysanthemum nozzle 81 and violet buttercream. Position the nozzle straight on to the cake with the curved part pointing away from the flower centre then gently squeeze the piping bag as you lift up and away slightly, releasing the pressure as you do so for each short petal. Pipe some short spikes in the centre using yellow.

9. Using light pink buttercream and flower nozzle 14, pipe the drop flowers by holding the piping bag at a 90-degree angle straight on to the cake, with the tip just touching the surface. Squeeze the piping bag as you gently turn it clockwise (counter-clockwise for left-handers) until it creates a flower then stop squeezing and pull the piping bag away. Add flower centres and simple petal strokes (see Piping Flowers) using yellow buttercream.

10. Add some dots and small leaves in between the flowers using light green buttercream. Use a piping bag with a small hole at the tip for the dots, and leaf nozzle 352 for the leaves.

HEAVENLY HAT BOX

A hat box may be just a simple container for carrying millinery to some people,
but we've elevated ours with the addition of soft pink and yellow roses to
give the impression of luxury. We've highlighted its classic look
by choosing a pale colour combination for the flowers that
perfectly compliments the pastel green of the box.

You will need

- 20cm (8in) round cake, 15cm (6in) high
- 15cm (6in) round cake, 5cm (2in) high
- 20cm (8in) round dummy cake, 2.5–4cm (1–1½in) high
- 20cm (8in) round thin cake board
- 700–800g (1lb 9oz–1lb 12oz) light green buttercream, to cover the cake (Sugarflair Spruce Green)
- 200–300g (7–10½oz) light pink buttercream (Sugarflair Dusky Pink)
- 200–300g (7–10½oz) pink buttercream (Sugarflair Dusky Pink)
- 200–300g (7–10½oz) yellow buttercream (Sugarflair Melon plus a hint of Autumn Leaf)
- 200–300g (7–10½oz) light green buttercream (Sugarflair Gooseberry)
- 200–300g (7–10½oz) light yellow buttercream (Sugarflair Caramel)
- Glue
- Scraper
- Serrated knife
- Dowel
- Sharpener
- Ruler
- Scissors
- Wilton petal nozzle 103
- Wilton petal nozzle 104
- Wilton leaf nozzle 352
- Piping bags
- Tweezers
- Pearl dragees (sugar balls)

1. Pre-pipe and freeze about 15 to 18 roses using the Wilton petal nozzle 104 and light pink, pink and yellow buttercream in a variety of sizes (see Piping Flowers).

2. Prepare the thin cake board and dummy cake that will become the box lid. Poke a hole in the centre of the board for a dowel to go through, before sticking the dummy cake to the non-laminated side of the board.

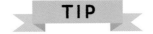

TIP

In this project we used a dummy cake for the lid to make it easier to assemble. However, you may use a real cake if you prefer.

3. Stack your 20cm (8in) cakes (see Buttercream Basics), then add the 15cm (6in) cake centrally to the top of the stack. Then carve the top cake diagonally. The highest point should allow enough space for the height of the roses that you will add here shortly. We found this to be about 5cm (2in) for our cake.

4. Insert a dowel down through the whole cake, measure and mark a point level with the highest point of the cake. Cut the dowel at your guide mark, pull it out and sharpen one end.

5. Place the dummy lid on the top of the cake to determine that it is the height you desire, then remove it. Crumb coat the cake and cover the lid and the cake sides with a smooth coat of light green buttercream (see Buttercream Basics).

6. Use a ruler or scraper to mark four straight equally spaced lines vertically around the cake.

7. Using light cream buttercream and the Wilton petal nozzle 103 with the wide end touching the guide mark, pipe two back to back ruffles (see Piping Textures), side by side without a gap in between, following your vertical guides.

8. Pipe blobs of buttercream to attach the roses to, and to increase the angle of their position if necessary. Make sure that the roses will not exceed the height of the centre cake so they do not get squashed when the lid goes on.

9. Pipe a very thin layer of buttercream on the top of the cake, insert the dowel with the pointed end upwards then put the lid on. Press it carefully but firmly so the dowel skewers the dummy cake and it will not come off.

10. Pipe a beads border (see Piping Textures) on the bottom edges of the cake lid and the top edge of the hat box in light green buttercream, using a piping bag with a small hole at the tip.

11. Pipe some leaves in light green between roses to cover the gaps using the Wilton leaf nozzle 352.

12. Continue the light cream ruffled lines up over the lid and then pipe a small ruffle flower (see Piping Flowers) where the ruffles intersect. Put some pearl dragees in the centre using tweezers to position them.

INSPIRED BY ROMERO BRITTO

Hailing from the bright and brilliant Brazilian neo-pop movement, Romero Britto is an artist, painter and sculptor whose work is a visual feast. We love his extraordinary skill at combining vibrant colours while infusing each piece with history, playful themes and pop art. He makes art that emanates love, cheerfulness and enthusiasm, so of course we were inspired!

You will need

- 20 x 15cm (8 x 6in) square cake, 15cm (6in) high
- 700g untinted buttercream
- 250g (9oz) black buttercream (Sugarflair Liquorice)
- 250g (9oz) yellow buttercream (Sugarflair Melon)
- 250g (9oz) dark yellow buttercream (Sugarflair Melon plus Autumn Leaf)
- 250g (9oz) orange buttercream (Sugarflair Tangerine)
- 250g (9oz) light pink buttercream (Sugarflair Claret)
- 250g (9oz) dusky pink buttercream (Sugarflair Tangerine)
- 250g (9oz) red buttercream (Sugarflair Christmas Red plus Ruby)
- 250g (9oz) light green buttercream (Sugarflair Gooseberry)
- 250g (9oz) medium dark green buttercream (Sugarflair Spruce Green)
- 250g (9oz) violet buttercream (Sugarflair Grape Violet)
- 250g (9oz) blue buttercream (Sugarflair Baby Blue)
- Wilton writing nozzle no.5
- Wilton round nozzle no.12
- Piping bags
- Cookie cutters (various sized hearts and small flowers)
- Cake scraper
- Cardboard templates for small circles and random shapes
- Cocktail sticks (toothpicks)

1. Prepare your tinted buttercream, bagging each colour in a separate piping bag with the tip cut off to create a small hole. For the black, you may use a Wilton writing nozzle no.5, or just cut the tip off a bag to make a slightly bigger hole.

2. Stack and crumb coat your cake (see Buttercream Basics). Then start by marking the position of the largest hearts first as they will be the main decorations. Use a cookie cutter to mark one on the top and two or three more on the sides.

TIP

To stop the black tinted buttercream bleeding into the other colours, you can pipe it first then let it crust for between 30 minutes and an hour before piping the rest of the pattern. The best way to mark your patterns is with various cutters, as you can change the design by smoothing them over until you are happy with the overall layout.

3. Using a cocktail stick (toothpick), start to mark the outline of some half circles on the bottom edge of all four sides of the cake.

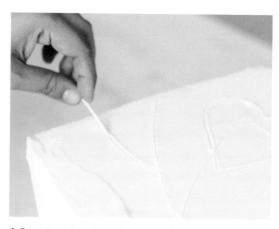

4. Draw long lines that will create a visually pleasing division all around the cake. To achieve the right effect these lines should connect with each other. Make sure that the spaces in between lines will be large enough to fit in more decorative shapes.

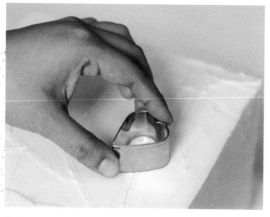

5. Using the smallest heart cookie cutter, mark some hearts randomly along the lines.

6. Using your black tinted buttercream, with continuous pressure, pipe on top of your long lines, then the big hearts and finally the smaller hearts.

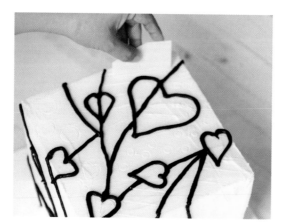

7. Using your Wilton round nozzle no.12, a flower cookie cutter, cake scraper and small cardboard templates, create patterns and stripes in between the long lines over the rest of the cake.

8. With repetitive back and forth movements and continuous and consistent pressure, fill in the smaller patterns (circles, hearts and flowers) in various colours. The motion will be like making embroidery stitches that vary in length and direction.

9. Now fill in the bigger spaces with stripes, making sure that you use all the different colours.

10. Finally cover the rest of the white space over the entire cake filling in all the shapes with stripes and solid colours, ensuring the direction of your 'stitches' vary from shape to shape.

VAN GOGH SUNFLOWERS

Van Gogh's sunflower paintings are surely the most globally recognisable examples of his art. The vibrancy of colour seems to have such a deep impact on the viewer. For us, Van Gogh's masterpiece is a symbol of optimism and hope.

You will need

- 20cm (8in) square cake, 10cm (4in) high
- 200–300g (7–10½oz) dark yellow buttercream (Sugarflair Autumn Leaf)
- 200–300g (7–10½oz) bright yellow buttercream (Sugarflair Melon plus Autumn Leaf)
- 200–300g (7–10½oz) medium yellow buttercream (Sugarflair Autumn Leaf plus a hint of Melon)
- 200–300g (7–10½oz) light blue buttercream (Sugarflair Baby Blue)
- 50–100g (1¾–3½oz) dark blue buttercream (Sugarflair Baby Blue)
- 100–200g (3½–7oz) dark green buttercream (Sugarflair Spruce Green)
- 100–200g (3½–7oz) light green buttercream (Sugarflair Spruce Green plus Gooseberry)
- 400–500g (14oz–1lb 2oz) dark brown buttercream (Sugarflair Dark Brown)
- 100–200g (3½–7oz) light brown buttercream (Sugarflair Dark Brown)
- Palette knife
- Small tip palette knife
- Baking (parchment) paper
- Pencil
- Scissors
- Piping bags
- Wilton small star nozzle 16
- Wilton leaf nozzle 67
- Wilton leaf nozzle 352

1. Apply dark yellow buttercream across the bottom part of the cake, creating the impression of a sloping 'landscape' to appear behind the flowers. Add some bright yellow buttercream, even it out with the larger palette knife and apply short horizontal strokes using the small tip palette knife.

2. Repeat the same process to cover the remaining surface of the cake using two shades of blue buttercream.

TIP

There is a wide variety of leaf nozzles available so experiment to find the perfect effect for your cake.

3. Cut a piece of baking (parchment) paper that is exactly the same height and width as the side of the cake. Fold the paper in half twice horizontally then mark the sides of the cake with a piece of card where the folds are.

4 Use the star nozzle 16 and dark brown buttercream to pipe tightly packed diagonal lines between your guide marks. Each subsequent row leans in the opposite direction. Make sure that there are no gaps in between.

5. Use the same star nozzle and pipe a scallop-like border all around the top edge of the cake.

6. Pipe the flower stems with dark green buttercream using a piping bag with a medium hole at the tip.

7. Position and mark all the sunflower heads by piping guide circles.

8. Pipe the sunflowers using leaf nozzle 67 (see Piping Flowers). Refer to the photograph of the finished cake as a guide, and pipe all the flowers that seem to be underneath or the lowest first, including the one on the side of the cake, before piping the rest.

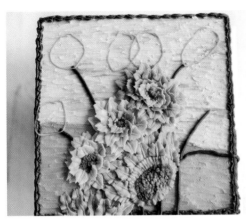

9. Build up the sunflowers and swap between the two darker shades of yellow buttercream as you do so, to create variety.

10. Complete the rest of the sunflower heads using leaf nozzle 352 and the bright yellow. When piping the petals here make them more narrow and flatter than the others. Pipe the centre of the flowers using dark and light brown buttercream dots.

IMPRESSION OF WATERLILIES

Using a simple piping technique it's remarkable how easy it is to achieve an impressionist masterpiece! Claude Monet's famous waterlily painting series was our inspiration, and buttercream our medium. Even without much detail, it is still perfectly clear that the subject is delicate pink water lilies on a tranquil pond.

You will need

- 20cm (8in) round cake, 15cm (6in) high
- 300–400g (10½–14oz) light blue buttercream (Sugarflair Navy Blue)
- 300–400g (10½–14oz) medium blue buttercream (Sugarflair Baby Blue plus Navy Blue)
- 300–400g (10½–14oz) dark blue buttercream (Sugarflair Navy Blue)
- 300–400g (10½–14oz) very light green buttercream (Sugarflair Gooseberry)
- 300–400g (10½–14oz) light green buttercream (Sugarflair Spruce Green)
- 300–400g (10½–14oz) medium green buttercream (Sugarflair Spruce Green plus Party Green)
- 300–400g (10½–14oz) dark green buttercream (Sugarflair Holly Green)
- 300–400g (10½–14oz) light pink buttercream (Sugarflair Claret)
- 50–100g (1¾–3½oz) dark pink buttercream (Sugarflair Claret)
- 50–100g (1¾–3½oz) dark purple buttercream (Sugarflair Grape Violet plus Claret)
- 50–100g (1¾–3½oz) yellow buttercream (Sugarflair Autumn Leaf)
- Wilton petal nozzle 125
- Wilton grass nozzle 233
- Wilton leaf nozzle 352
- Piping bags
- Coupler

1. When piping the basic 'impressionist dots' with the grass nozzle 233, hold the piping bag straight on to the surface of the cake at a 90-degree angle before squeezing the piping bag.

2. Squeeze the piping bag gently until the buttercream builds up slightly, then stop squeezing the bag before pulling away.

TIP

If you accidentally squeeze the piping bag too much and the small dots became too fat and look like they are merging, just scrape them off with a palette knife or scraper, then pipe again.

3. Stack the cakes, carve the curved top edge (see Wedgewood Blue cake, steps 1–4), then crumb coat (see Buttercream Basics). Use any of the shades of blue buttercream in a piping bag with a small hole at the tip and mark the position for all the different blues.

4. Pipe all the shades of blue buttercream using the grass nozzle 233. When piping the details, make sure they are in clusters and not dotted about, so the colours will not get blended together.

5. Continue to pipe guide lines to mark out areas for the shades of green.

6. Repeat the process as for the blues, and add all the different shades of green except for the darkest shade.

7. Using a piping bag with a small hole at the tip, add some dark green accents by piping wavy rows of dots that are close to each other.

8. Repeat the same process using plain buttercream, light and dark pink, and dark purple to give the impression of some water lilies.

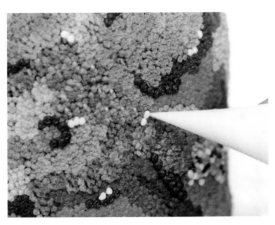

9. Add a few white dots randomly, again using a piping bag with a small hole at the tip, in order to create highlights.

10. Pipe some lily pads on top of the cake using petal nozzle 125. Hold the piping bag at a flattish angle with the surface of the cake, with the wide end at the centre. Continuously squeeze the piping bag as you turn your bag clockwise.

11. Pipe the lilies in the centre of the lily pads using light pink buttercream as if you were piping a sunflower (see Piping Flowers), making sure that the petals start with a steep angle of 30 to 40 degrees, increasing the angle as you pipe towards the centre of the flower.

12. Add centre spikes using yellow buttercream and a piping bag with a small hole at the tip. Pipe more pads and lilies at the base of the cake.

TOILE DE JOUY

Toile de jouy is a classic decoration originally used on textiles, and was popular in the mid-18th century. Small floral or pastoral scenes are repeated over and over in a single colour. You can choose to depict whatever you like, either by tracing onto baking (parchment) paper or by using die-cut paper designs, doilies and paper appliqués. As you can see, with simple repeated images you can achieve a really sophisticated look.

You will need

- 20 x 20cm (8 x 8in) square cake, 4in (10cm) high
- 1.5kg (3lb 5oz) white buttercream (Sugarflair Super White powder)
- Pink food colouring paste (Sugarflair Dusky Pink)
- Baking (parchment) paper
- Pen or pencil
- Scissors
- Small piece of cardboard or stiff paper
- Ruler
- Scraper

- Serrated knife
- Dinky Doodle Pearl airbrush paint
- Paint palette or dish
- Paint brush, any size
- Small bowl of water
- Clean sponge
- Clean tissue
- Cocktail stick (toothpick)
- Piping bags
- Wilton nozzle 199

1. Trace your chosen image onto baking (parchment) paper, or find a nice royalty-free image on the internet and resize it until it fits your design. Cut out the shapes.

2. Stack your cake (see Buttercream basics). Cut a right-angle triangle from cardboard or paper with the two short sides measuring 5cm (2in). Make four of these triangles. Position each one at the corners of the cake as a guide.

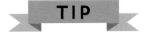

TIP

The only limitation on the designs you choose is your own imagination!
You can draw your own or search the internet for royalty-free images,
or even seek out the kind of cut-outs used for scrapbooking.

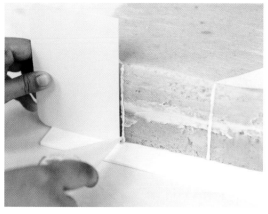

3. Using a scraper or a ruler, mark the sides of the cake from the tips of the triangles, down to the base using any colour of buttercream in a piping bag with the tip cut off.

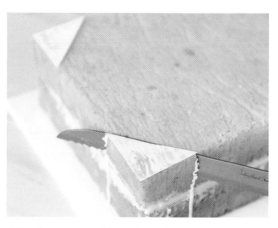

4. Cut the corners of the cake straight down with the serrated knife, then crumb coat the cake and cover with a smooth coat of white buttercream (see Buttercream Basics).

5. Position your paper design pieces onto the cake straight away after covering it, so that they adhere to the slightly sticky buttercream. If the surface has crusted too much and the design does not stick to the cake, dab a thin layer of vegetable shortening to the paper.

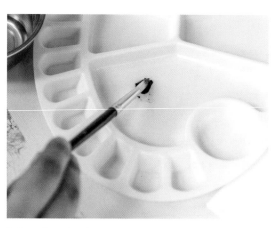

6. Put a little pink food colouring paste onto a paint palette or dish and add few drops of water to dilute it. Use a brush to make sure you dissolve the paste properly.

7. Cut a small piece of sponge, dip it into the colour and remove any excess. Dab it onto a clean tissue to remove the excess water and to check the strength of colour.

8. Dab the surface of the cake gently. Add more colour around the pattern to give a shadow effect and add depth.

9. Mix a paler shade for the background and continue dabbing it onto the cake.

10. Use a cocktail stick (toothpick) to lift and gently remove the design stencils from the cake.

11. Pipe loops as border around the bottom of the cake using Wilton nozzle 199.

TIP

When applying the colour, make sure you don't dab too heavily so you don't leave dents on the cake.

WEDGEWOOD BLUE

The iconic colour of Wedgewood jasperware pottery is famous around the world. The soft background blue is decorated with often floral decoration of great delicacy. You can create a charming little historical piece by adding your own monochromatic 'Wedgewood' design to a cake. Your design can be any pattern that you fancy – choose something suitable and your cake will simply exude sophistication.

You will need

- 20cm (8in) round cake, 15cm (6in) high
- 1kg (2lb 4oz) light blue buttercream to cover the cake (Sugarflair Navy Blue plus a hint of Baby Blue)
- 100–200g (3½–7oz) light blue buttercream (Sugarflair Navy Blue plus a hint of Baby Blue)
- 100–200g (3½–7oz) medium blue buttercream (Sugarflair Navy Blue)
- 100–200g (3½–7oz) of dark blue buttercream (Sugarflair Navy Blue)
- Baking (parchment) paper
- Scissors

- Pen or pencil
- Ruler
- Serrated knife
- Small piece of paper or cardboard
- Scraper
- Piping bags
- Wilton writing nozzles no.2 or 3 (optional)
- Paint brushes, flat and rounded tip
- Small bowl of water
- Cocktail stick (toothpick)

1. Stack your cake (see Buttercream Basics), then make a circle of baking (parchment) paper 2.5cm (1in) smaller all round than the top of the cake.

2. Depending on how curved you want the edges to be, measure about 2.5–5cm (1–2in) down from the top edge of the cake and mark a guide line in buttercream all the way around.

TIP

Some types of Wedgewood pottery have blue details on a white background, which would make a lovely variation. Or you could use just one shade of blue for your piping, or even more shades than we have.

3. Start carving the edge of the cake carefully into a nice curve following the paper and the mark.

4. On a piece of cardboard, draw the desired curve shape and use this as a guide to check the preciseness and consistency of your curved edge. Trim more cake if necessary to adjust the curve.

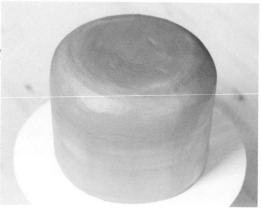

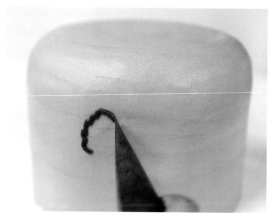

5. After you have achieved the curved edge, crumb coat and cover the cake with a smooth coat of light blue buttercream (see Buttercream basics).

6. Prepare three shades of blue buttercream, light, medium and dark, in separate piping bags with the tips cut off, or with Wilton writing nozzles no.2 or 3. Starting at the outer edge of your first petal, pipe an uneven line of medium blue as an outline.

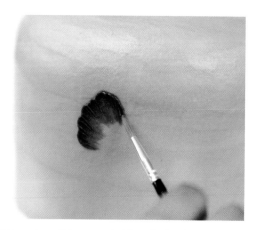

7. Using a damp flat or rounded tip paint brush, sweep the buttercream down from the outline towards the centre or base of the flower. Repeat the process for a couple more outer petals.

8. Repeat the same process, piping and brushing layers of petals until you complete the whole flower. Pipe the outline again to make it slightly thicker if you have brushed it too much.

9. Outline where you want the leaves and stems to go using a cocktail stick (toothpick).

10. Use light blue buttercream to fill the leaves. Pipe zigzag motion like embroidery stitching (see the Inspired by Romero Britto cake, step 8).

11. Use dark blue buttercream and the same piping motion to outline the leaves and to pipe the stems.

12. Add more flowers all around the cake, in a variety of sizes, then finish with a dark blue piped shell or beads border (see Piping Textures) around the bottom.

BAS RELIEF

Inspired by a form of sculpture in which shapes are carved from a flat surface so that they stand up from the backround, this is our buttercream take on bas relief. Our detailed design is piped onto the background, rather than being carved out of it, and you could choose a light or dark surface colour to show the details off. Ornate yet sophisticated, this cake is is perfect for life's big celebrations.

You will need

- 15 x 15cm (6 x 6in) square cake, 20cm (8in) high
- 1kg (2lb 4oz) light cream buttercream (Sugarflair Caramel)
- 800g (1lb 12oz) medium cream buttercream (Sugarflair Caramel)
- Dowels
- Scraper
- Piping bags

- Scissors
- Coupler
- Wilton petal nozzle 103
- Wilton small star nozzle 16
- Wilton writing nozzle no.1 (optional)
- Airbrush machine
- Pearl airbrush colour

1. Stack and dowel the cake to stabilize it, then crumb coat and cover with a smooth coat of medium cream buttercream (see Buttercream Basics).

2. Using medium cream buttercream and the Wilton petal nozzle 103, pipe the buds, roses and ruffle flowers (see Piping Flowers) on all the corners of the cake.

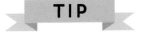

TIP

Besides the piped details that give you the elegant bas relief effect, you can also use a variety of moulds to make features to stick to the cake with a thin layer of buttercream (see Moulds). If the moulded designs are heavy you will find that piping gel or edible glue may not be strong enough to keep them from falling off the cake.

3. When the flowers have crusted, gently pat down the rough parts where your piping strokes ended.

4. Using medium cream buttercream in a piping bag with a small hole at the tip, pipe a calyx on each of the buds and roses and dots on the base of the ruffle flowers.

5. Using the Wilton small star nozzle 16, fill the gaps around the roses and buds with stars, with some extending on both sides to look like long flowers. Make sure you cover all gaps in between the flowers with small stars.

6. Add small buds at the tip of the long star flowers. Pipe some small buds in layers using just a piping bag with a small hole at the tip, or Wilton writing nozzle no.1.

7. Pipe some scrolls randomly around the corners of the cake to add pretty detail.

8. Airbrush some details using pearl colour to highlight some flowers. Don't overdo it – you just want to add a little sparkle, not to make the cake look too metallic.

TIP

When airbrushing colour onto small details, make sure you bring the spray gun closer to allow the spray to reach the finer details, but be careful not to get so close that the colour pools on the surface and drips.

TOTALLY TROPICAL

Relax into the island-style vibe of this tropically inspired cake. Bamboo and hibiscus combine to create a fresh, serene design that's perfect for an outdoor summer celebration, the cascade of exotic flowers adding some hot colour against the calm green background.

You will need

- 15cm (6in) square cake, 10cm (4in) high
- 600–700g (1lb 5oz–1lb 9oz) green buttercream (Sugarflair Gooseberry)
- 50–100g (1¾–3½oz) caramel buttercream (Sugarflair Caramel)
- 100–200g (3½–7oz) yellow buttercream (Sugarflair Autumn Leaf)
- 150–200g (5½–7oz) white buttercream (Sugarflair Super White powder)
- 100–200g (3½–7oz) light pink (Sugarflair Claret)
- 100–200g (3½–7oz) orange buttercream (Sugarflair Apricot)
- 100–200g (3½–7oz) blue buttercream (Sugarflair Baby Blue plus Navy Blue)
- Wilton writing nozzle no.10
- Wilton petal nozzle 104
- Wafer paper leaves
- Piping bags

1. When piping the bamboo, hold the piping bag to the side, in the direction you are piping, to achieve the rounded shape of each bamboo segment (top). Do not hold it at 90 degrees to the cake's surface as the bamboo will look flat (bottom).

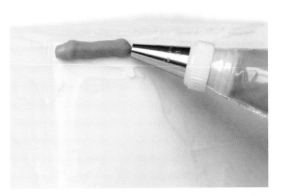

2. Stack and crumb coat your cake (see Buttercream Basics). Then starting at any top corner on any side of the cake, pipe bamboo segments in green buttercream using the writing nozzle no.10, and vary them from 2.5cm (1in) to 4cm (1½in) in length.

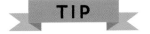

TIP

This cake is a rectangular block on its side. Because the cake is small, we did not use any dowels for support but if you want to make yours taller, you should of course add dowels to stabilize the layers.

3. Use caramel buttercream in a piping bag with a small hole at the tip, and pipe a short but thick line after each bamboo segment.

4. Repeat the same process to pipe the bamboo all around the edges of the cake, and then work inwards until you have covered each surface of the cake.

5. Make sure that the lines of bamboo are tightly packed so that they do not have gaps in between them.

6. Pipe the frangipani flowers directly on to the cake in white and yellow buttercream using the Two-tone Effect described in the Lace Romance cake, and the petal nozzle 104 (see Piping Flowers). Some of them can overlap so the effect is more natural.

7. Make the wafer paper leaves (see Using Wafer Paper in the techniques section). Pipe a blob of buttercream where you want the leaves to be positioned.

8. Position and insert the wafer paper leaves and arrange them according to how you want them.

9. Pipe the orange hibiscus flowers directly on to the cake using nozzle 104, and add the centre dots in yellow (see Piping Flowers). Make sure you use a little pressure when piping so that the flowers adhere to the cake properly.

10. Add some pink hibiscus for extra colour and to complete the cake.

BEACH TREASURE

The sight of the ocean never fails to impress, and the shoreline has a special power to draw us to it. So what could be more appealing than a beach-inspired cake? Especially one with the hint of buried pirate treasure! We have included edible sea shells, biscuit crumb sand and blue ruffle waves, and even piped a length of discarded rope and a compass – a treat for beachcombers, sailors and all beach lovers.

You will need

- 20cm (8in) round cake, 15cm (6in) high
- 1kg (2lb 4oz) light cream buttercream (Sugarflair Caramel)
- 400–500g (14oz–1lb 2oz) medium blue buttercream (Sugarflair Baby Blue plus Navy Blue)
- 400–500g (14oz–1lb 2oz) light blue buttercream (Sugarflair Navy Blue)
- 300–400g (10½–14oz) white buttercream (Sugarflair Super White powder)
- 100–200g (3½–7oz) dark yellow buttercream (Sugarflair Autumn Leaf)
- 50–100g (1¾–3½oz) black buttercream (Sugarflair Liquorice)
- 50–100g (1¾–3½oz) brown buttercream (Sugarflair Dark Brown)
- 30–50g (1¼–1¾oz) red buttercream (Sugarflair Ruby Red)

- Scraper
- Palette knife
- Piping bags
- Scissors
- Non-woven cloth
- 2–3 tbsps cocoa powder
- Small bowl of water
- 3–4 tbsps melted cocoa butter or vegetable shortening
- Paint palette or small saucer
- Round-tip paint brush
- Rounded square-tip paint brush
- Cocktail stick (toothpick)
- Wilton petal nozzle 104
- Crushed digestive biscuits (graham crackers)

1. Stack and crumb coat your cake (see Buttercream Basics), place it on the cake board then cover the cake with light cream buttercream, evening it out with a scraper. Using a piping bag with a hole at the tip, apply random small blobs of dark yellow buttercream then spread with a palette knife in a circular motion. Repeat with brown.

2. Scrape the side and top to give a marbled effect on the surface. Clean the scraper from time to time so the colours do not blend too much.

3. When the surface is even, use the non-woven cloth to smooth the surface of the cake very lightly. You should leave some rough areas around the cake.

4. Prepare your cocoa paint by dissolving the cocoa powder in the melted vegetable shortening or cocoa butter. Regulate the amount of cocoa powder you use depending on how dark you want the shade of brown to be.

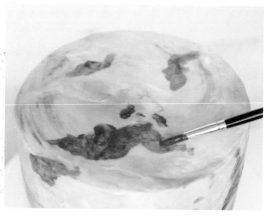

5. Use the round-tip paint brush to paint some patches of brown and then smudge the colour randomly to create an old and distressed look.

6. Use a cocktail stick (toothpick) to mark where you will pipe the waves.

7. Pipe the waves using petal nozzle 104 with white and medium blue buttercream, (see Two-tone Effect in the Lace Romance cake) with the wide end of the nozzle touching the cake and the narrow end pointing up and at a 20-degree angle.

8. Squeeze with even pressure as you move your hand slightly up and down and drag the wave down following your guide. Then dampen the tip of the rounded square-tip paint brush with water and sweep the blue buttercream downwards.

9. Repeat the same process switching between the two shades of blue to pipe waves all over the lower part of the cake and onto the cake board, following your guide mark.

10. Sprinkle the crushed biscuits all around the board and in between the waves. You can use the tip of the palette knife to sprinkle biscuit crumbs into narrow spaces.

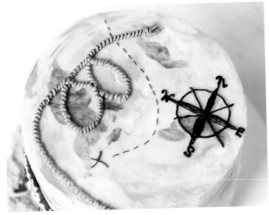

11. Add the ropes in light brown by piping short overlapping 'S' shapes to create a twisted rope pattern using a piping bag with a small hole at the tip. Pipe the map markings using a piping bag with a small hole at the tip and brown buttercream. Make the 'X' mark in red and the compass details in black.

12. Pipe 15 to 20 seashells using a piping bag with a medium hole at the tip (see Tip). Squeeze the piping bag with even pressure starting with the tip touching the surface, then move your hand in a round motion as the shell gets bigger.

TIP

When piping the seashells, you can also use a Wilton writing nozzle no.2 or 3, or even small star nozzles like Wilton 14 or 16. Alternatively, you can even go bigger than that depending on the size you want. You can also freeze the shells first before applying them, because it can be challenging to pipe them directly onto the crumbled biscuits.

COUNTRY WINDOW

Imagine yourself in a country house surrounded by a beautiful garden, with stunning views of meadows and greenery beyond. Even the experience of making this cake, and certainly seeing the finished results, will fill you with a sense of tranquility.

You will need

- 20cm (8in) square cake, 10cm (4in) high
- 100–150g (3½–5½oz) white buttercream (Sugarflair Super White powder)
- 700–800g (1lb 9oz–1lb 12oz) medium caramel buttercream (Sugarflair Caramel)
- 300–400g (10½–14oz) light caramel buttercream (Sugarflair Caramel)
- 100–200g (3½–7oz) dark yellow buttercream (Sugarflair Autumn Leaf)
- 100–150g (3½–5½oz) blue buttercream (Sugarflair Baby Blue plus Navy Blue)
- 100–150g (3½–5½oz) light green tinted buttercream (Sugarflair Gooseberry)
- 100–150g (3½–5½oz) medium green buttercream (Sugarflair Spruce Green)
- 100–150g (3½–5½oz) dark green buttercream (Sugarflair Holly Green)
- 100–150g (3½–5½oz) light pink buttercream (Sugarflair Claret)
- 100–150g (3½–5½oz) dark pink buttercream (Sugarflair Claret)
- 100–150g (3½–5½oz) grey buttercream (Sugarflair Liquorice)
- 100–150g (3½–5½oz) black buttercream (Sugarflair Liquorice)
- 100–150g (3½–5½oz) light brown buttercream (Sugarflair Dark Brown)
- 100–150g (3½–5½oz) dark brown buttercream (Sugarflair Dark Brown)
- Pen or pencil
- Baking (parchment) paper
- Scissors
- Serrated knife
- Piping bags
- Palette knife
- Scraper
- Non-woven cloth
- Brick embosser
- Rounded square-tip paint brush
- Sugarflair Autumn Leaf food colouring paste
- Paint palette
- Small bowl of water
- Cocktail stick (toothpick)
- Wilton small star nozzle 14
- Wilton petal nozzle 103
- Wilton basketweave nozzle 47

1. Cut a window template out of baking (parchment) paper that is 15cm (6in) wide and 25cm (10in) long, making the top part rounded like an arch. Place it on top of your cake and cut around it using a serrated knife. Attach the excess cake at the bottom to make the window length longer. Level the surface of the cake by trimming it, if necessary (we found we could just cover the whole cake as is).

2. Crumb coat the cake (see Buttercream Basics), then cover the top with white and the sides with medium caramel buttercream. Apply random blobs of dark yellow on the side of the cake and blend with a palette knife in a circular motion.

3. After blending, use the scraper to blend the colours even more. Scrape the cake in both directions (right to left, and left to right).

4. Pipe random small blobs of blue buttercream at the arched end, and blend them into the background in a circular motion. This will create the 'clouds' effect for the sky. Next, gently scrape using the scraper, in both directions. Then lightly smooth the surface of the whole cake with a non-woven cloth (see Buttercream Basics).

5. Press the brick embosser firmly onto the sides of the cake. To give an old and weathered look, dilute Autumn Leaf food colouring paste with water and lightly brush the surface of the embosser before pressing. Do not brush with too much water.

6. Using the basketweave nozzle 47 and light caramel buttercream, pipe an outline all around the top edge of the cake, with the smooth side of the nozzle pointing upwards. Pipe three layers altogether, one on top of the other, to make the window frame.

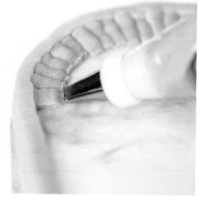

7. Even out the 'join' of the two colours on the side of the cake with a small palette knife.

8. Pipe an inner frame of 2.5cm (1in) long strips all round the window, using the same nozzle and the light caramel buttercream. Pipe two more rows of strips across the bottom of the window, on top of the frame and on the outer edge, where the frame meets the brick pattern.

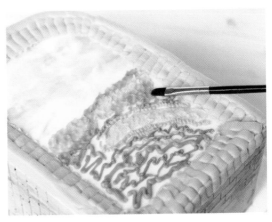

9. Pipe half the horizon and the path using light caramel buttercream, then use a damp paint brush and gently make a tapping motion to create texture.

10. Use the different shades of green buttercream, and pipe them onto the cake to create the meadows effect. Do not pipe the buttercream too thickly. Repeat the tapping motion to blend the colours together.

11. Add the impression of some water in the landscape using blue buttercream, and add some shadows with dark green. You can also add mountains and trees, and blend them with a brush or just leave them piped.

12. Pipe blobs of grey buttercream at the bottom of the scene to create the impression of rocks, and pipe streaks of black buttercream on their surface as shadows, lightly blending them with a brush.

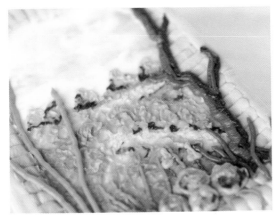

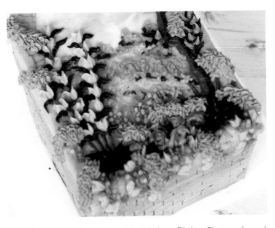

13. Pipe some stems and vines using different shades of green, and also the tree and branches using light and dark brown buttercream.

14. Pipe the buds using light pink (see Piping Flowers), and small dots using light and dark pink. Pipe foliage using the small star nozzle 14 in medium green. For the smaller leaves, cut a slightly bigger hole at the tip of the piping bag and pipe spikes and wavy spikes with two shades of green.

RIBBON ROSE HEART

As their name suggests, these roses are formed from a piped ribbon of buttercream and are so easy to create yet very effective. Start with a plain white background as a simple canvas, and with a delicate touch you can elevate your cake to a different level where it radiates elegance and style. You can arrange the roses into any shape you wish, in this case we went for a classic romantic statement by forming a heart.

You will need

- 15cm (6in) round cake, 10cm (4in) high
- 600–750g (1lb 5oz–1lb 10oz) white buttercream (Sugarflair Super White powder)
- 200–300g (7–10½oz) pink buttercream (Sugarflair Claret)
- 200–300g (7–10½oz) red buttercream (Sugarflair Claret, Orange and Ruby Red)
- Baking (parchment) paper
- Scissors
- Flower nail

- Wilton petal nozzle 103
- Piping bags
- Cocktail stick (toothpick)
- Scraper
- Cake board or tray
- Tweezers
- Pearl dragees (sugar balls)

1. Cut small baking (parchment) paper squares. Pipe a blob of buttercream on to the flower nail and stick on one parchment paper square.

2. Using the Wilton petal nozzle 103 with red buttercream, pipe a ribbon rose by holding the nozzle upright with the wide end touching the flower nail. Squeeze continuously as you turn your flower nail.

TIP

The ribbon roses are small and made of only a little buttercream so they melt easily, especially when you are applying them to the cake and they are in contact with your fingers. When they start to soften, just put them back in the freezer. Make sure you pipe fresh buttercream on the cake surface so the roses adhere better, and use a cocktail stick (toothpick) to help you press them on firmly.

3. Use scissors and lift the piped ribbon roses onto a tray or board then put them in the freezer for few minutes to harden. Repeat to make about 40 to 50 roses in red and pink buttercream.

4. Stack, crumb coat and cover the cake with a smooth coat using 500–600g (1lb 2oz–1lb 5oz) of the white buttercream (see Buttercream Basics). Reserve the rest for steps 5 and 9. Mark the outline shape for your design onto the cake surface using a cocktail stick (toothpick).

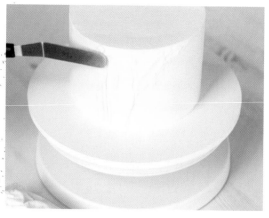

5. Apply white buttercream on the surface area that you want to attach the ribbon roses to.

6. Take the frozen ribbon roses from the freezer and quickly position and stick them to the surface of the cake. To do this without touching them – so they don't melt so easily – use cocktail sticks, poking on both sides and wiggling them as you press down.

7. Start at any side of your design and work towards the centre. Alternate the pink and red roses for variety.

8. Repeat the same process and apply the roses on the top surface of the cake following your outline.

9. Put white buttercream in a piping bag with a small hole cut at the tip and apply into the gaps between and around the ribbon roses.

10. Use tweezers to add the small pearl dragees and fill the gaps.

LACE ROMANCE

By piping delicate lace patterning onto a white background, it's possible to achieve an elegant and romantic cake design. You could choose to make your lace more dense or sparser depending on the look you want to achieve. In fact, creating variations in the density of the lace will actually make the whole design even more effective, creating dark and light areas of the surface. Add a few flowers and you'll have a cake with real impact.

You will need

- 15cm (6in) square cake, 20cm (8in) high
- 1kg (2lb 4oz) white buttercream (Sugarflair Super White powder)
- 300–400g (10½–14oz) black buttercream (Sugarflair Liquorice)
- 200–300g (7–10½oz) green buttercream (Sugarflair Gooseberry)
- 200–300g (7–10½oz) orange buttercream (Sugarflair Tangerine plus a hint of Liquorice)
- 200–300g (7–10½oz) purple buttercream (Sugarflair Grape Violet plus a hint of Liquorice)
- 200–300g (7–10½oz) yellow buttercream (Sugarflair Melon plus a hint of Autumn Leaf and a hint of Liquorice)
- Scraper
- Wilton writing nozzle no.1
- Wilton leaf nozzle 352
- Wilton petal nozzle 104
- Piping bags
- Scissors

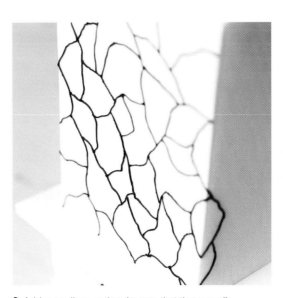

1. Stack and crumb coat the cake, then cover with a smooth coat of white buttercream (see Buttercream Basics). Using black buttercream with the Wilton writing nozzle no.1, pipe random short and slightly wavy lines.

2. Add more lines and make sure that they are all connected from one point to another. Repeat the same process until the cake is fully decorated with black lace piping effect.

TIP

Make sure that the tip of your nozzle is always touching the surface of the cake, and never pull it away from the cake as the line might either break or curl up. If this accidentally happens, first try to mend it by joining the broken line to another point. If that's not possible because the line of buttercream has curled up, pipe shorter lines around it so that it is not very obvious.

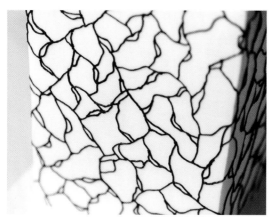

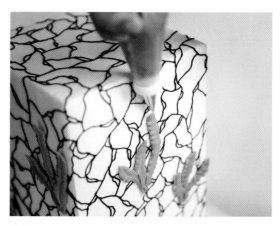

3. Pipe shorter wavy lines randomly, but still connected to your lace web, to add more eye-catching texture.

4. Decide where you want to position your flowers. Using green buttercream, pipe long and wavy leaves for the flowers using the Wilton leaf nozzle 352.

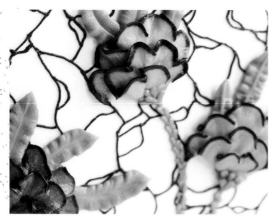

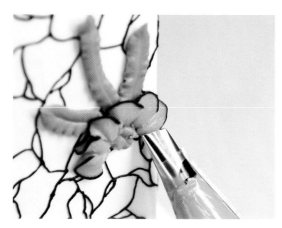

5. Next pipe the flowers using two-tone buttercream (see 'To make the two-tone effect').

6. Start creating the flowers by piping four or five simple petals (see Piping Flowers) in a half circle positioned at the base of the leaves you piped earlier.

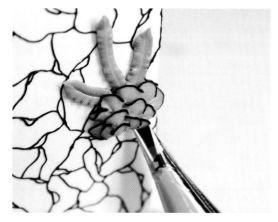

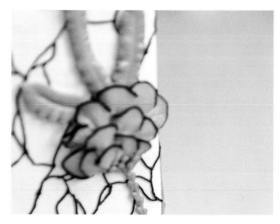

7. Pipe two or three layers of petals below the first, making sure that the number of petals decreases as you pipe towards the base of the flower. Repeat to create more flowers using the other buttercream colours.

8. Pipe the calyx and the stem for each of the flowers using green buttercream in a piping bag with a small hole at the tip. The stem is created by piping repeating small teardrop 'v' shapes.

To make the two-tone effect

a

Fill two piping bags with your two chosen colours, one colour in each bag. Attach the Wilton petal nozzle 104 to a third empty piping bag. Cut the tips off the two filled piping bags, but make the hole for the 'stripe' colour smaller than the main colour.

b

Pipe a line of the stripe colour of buttercream inside the empty piping bag, aligning it with the narrow end of the nozzle.

c

The other colour will need a bigger hole in its piping bag. Pipe this colour on top of the stripe colour to fill the bag.

d

Squeeze the piping bag until you get the desired two-tone effect. Turn the nozzle if you want the stripe thicker or thinner.

BALL OF FLOWERS

Flowers can be words in the language of love, and roses are without doubt the most traditional way to express affection. How would you arrange a basket of blooms to best convey your message? Just imagine presenting this delicate ball of flowers cake with a handwritten note – such a heart-warming gift.

You will need

- Two 15cm (6in) half dome cakes
- 500–600g (1lb 2oz–1lb 5oz) plain buttercream (for blobs and roses)
- 200–300g (7–10½oz) caramel buttercream (Sugarflair Caramel)
- 100–200g (3½–7oz) light brown buttercream (Sugarflair Dark Brown)
- 100–200g (3½–7oz) dark brown buttercream (Sugarflair Dark Brown)
- 300–400g (10½–14oz) red-violet buttercream (Sugarflair Grape Violet plus Claret)
- 300–400g (10½–14oz) dark red-violet buttercream (Sugarflair Grape Violet)
- 300–400g (10½–14oz) dusky pink buttercream (Sugarflair Dusky Pink)
- 300–400g (10½–14oz) pink buttercream (Sugarflair Claret)
- 100–200g (3½–7oz) green buttercream (Sugarflair Gooseberry)

- 15cm (6in) round, 5cm (2in) thick styrofoam board
- 20cm (8in) round, 2.5cm (1in) thick styrofoam board
- Flower nail
- Baking (parchment) paper
- Wilton petal nozzle 104
- Wilton petal nozzle 103
- Piping bags
- Printout, gift wrapper or scrapbook paper
- Contact paper or clear sticky backed plastic
- Scissors
- Glue
- Dowel
- Matching ribbons
- Cocktail stick (toothpick)

1. Pipe and freeze the small roses and ruffle flowers ahead of time (see Piping Flowers) using red-violet, dark red-violet, pink, dusky pink and plain buttercream, and the petal nozzle 104 for the roses, and 103 for the ruffle flowers. Some of the roses use the Two-tone Effect, which can be found in the instructions for the Lace Romance cake.

2. Prepare the styrofoam boards by cutting out a suitable design from a printout, gift wraping or scrapbook paper, then glue it to both of the styrofoam boards and cover with contact paper or clear sticky backed plastic. Cover the sides of the boards with matching ribbon then stick them together.

3. Before filling and crumb coating the cake, cut a piece off the rounded top of one of the cake domes so it will sit flat on a board. Apply a thin layer of buttercream on the cake so it sticks to the board.

4. Sandwich the two domes together with a buttercream filling between them, then crumb coat the resulting ball of cake (see Buttercream Basics). Place the ball centrally on top of the styrofoam board stack and insert a long dowel all the way through to the bottom styrofoam board to secure the cake.

5. Pipe the basketweave using brown, light brown and caramel buttercream. Use a piping bag with a medium hole at the tip and pipe two short strokes to create slightly overlapping and off-set 'V' shapes in rows around the cake. Cover more than half the cake and make sure there are no gaps in between the weaves.

6. When putting the roses and ruffle flowers onto the cake, make sure you pipe a blob of fresh buttercream onto the surface and press the flower firmly to the cake. This is to make sure that they adhere to the cake properly, especially as they are on the curved sides and will be inclined to slip off.

TIP

Roses and other similar flowers are created with quite a lot of buttercream and therefore they can be a little heavy. Due to the weight, these flowers ideally need to be positioned where there are supporting corners or edges. Since this is a sphere cake with no corners at all, it's best to stick the roses and ruffle flowers just above the 'equator' of your sphere so they will not slide down.

7. Insert a cocktail stick (toothpick) into both sides of the pre-piped frozen flowers in order to push them down onto the buttercream blobs securely, to make sure that they stick properly.

8. Pipe guide marks to determine the size of the rest of the flowers. Because the cake is small you want to plan the layout, positioning the flowers well, without gaps between. The dahlias are piped directly onto the cake. Alternate the two shades of violet and use petal nozzle 104 to pipe short spike-like petals in concentric circles.

9. Position the rest of the flowers, completing one layer after the other until you reach the top of the cake.

10. Using a piping bag with a small hole at the tip, pipe clusters of green buttercream blobs, like big dots, to represent buds. Next, with a piping bag with a smaller hole, insert the tip of the bag inside each green blob and fill with white buttercream until it shows on the surface.

11. Pipe clusters of small dots randomly using white buttercream to create the effect of delicate sprays of Baby's-breath (Gypsophila).

AUTUMN WREATH

This autumnal wreath has a certain rough-hewn charm that makes it very appealing.
The rugged twigs that intertwine each other highlight the natural beauty of the other
elements: the scattering of yellow, orange and red flowers, which together with
a few pine cones, berries, foliage and other natural adornments combine
to make such a rich display. It is perfect for welcoming the season!

You will need

- 25cm (10in) round cake, 10cm (4in) high
- 1kg (2lb 4oz) light brown buttercream (Sugarflair Dark Brown)
- 300g (10½oz) medium brown buttercream (Wilton Brown)
- 500g (1lb 2oz) dark brown buttercream (Sugarflair Dark Brown)
- 100–200g (3½–7oz) green buttercream (Sugarflair Gooseberry)
- 100–200g (3½–7oz) red buttercream (Sugarflair Christmas Red plus Ruby)
- 250g (9oz) cream buttercream (Sugarflair Cream)
- 250g (9oz) dark yellow buttercream (Sugarflair Autumn Leaf plus Melon)
- 250g (9oz) dark orange buttercream (Sugarflair Tangerine plus Ruby)

- 250g (9oz) orange buttercream (Sugarflair Tangerine)
- Wilton petal nozzle 102
- Wilton petal nozzle 104
- Wilton petal nozzle 352
- Wilton leaf nozzle 74
- Wilton writing nozzle no.5
- Piping bags
- Baking (parchment) paper
- Scissors
- Pen or pencil
- Serrated knife
- Bread sticks or thick straight pretzels
- Cocktail stick (toothpick)

1. Draw a circle 2.5–5cm (1–2in) smaller than the actual size of your cake on baking (parchment) paper to use as a guide for cutting.

2. Using a serrated knife, held vertically downwards, cut the cake following your guide. Slide your fingers underneath and carefully push the centre up and pull it away.

TIP

For the excess/cutout part of the cake, you can decorate it like a small cake to match your wreath or make it into cakepops. For the pinecones, if you find it hard to pipe on a breadstick, you may prefer to pipe them as you would the roses and freeze, before arranging them on the cake.

3. Carve the edges of the cake to make it more rounded, then crumb coat (see Buttercream Basics) using light brown buttercream.

4. Prepare three shades of brown buttercream in separate piping bags, with the tip cut off to create a medium-size hole or with a Wilton writing nozzle no.5.

5. Start piping from the inner part of the wreath, working over the top edge then cover the outer side as you go round. Use more of the lightest brown and occasionally swap to the other two colours. Pipe the twigs in sections rather than just going all round the cake in one colour.

6. Pipe the pine cones onto a bread stick in dark brown buttercream with the Wilton petal nozzle 102, using the Rose piping technique (see Piping Flowers) but keeping all the 'petals' short. If you find this challenging, you can freeze the pinecones instead, as you would a rose.

7. Build up the pinecone with more layers of 'petals' until it looks rounded.

8. Position each pinecone and stick the breadstick into the cake to hold it in place. You can use a cocktail stick (toothpick) to help the breadstick into the cake.

86

9. Use plain buttercream to pipe some blobs to determine the position of the flowers and to give them something to sit on to get them at the right angle.

10. Pipe the flowers as follows: the camellias in cream using Wilton petal nozzle 104 (see Ruffle Flowers four and five) with yellow and green centre spikes; then the orange and dark orange flowers using the Wilton leaf nozzle 74, and sunflowers in dark yellow and dark brown using the Wilton petal nozzle 352 (see Piping Flowers for both).

11. Pipe some leaves in green using the Wilton petal nozzle 352 and make sure that there are no big gaps left between the flowers.

12. Pipe the branches for the berries in dark brown buttercream, using a piping bag with a medium-size hole at the tip, then pipe the berries using the Wilton writing nozzle no.5 with red buttercream. If there are any unsightly peaks, wait until the buttercream is crusted and just press them down with a finger.

TERRARIUM

Here we have used a terrarium, not to hold small plants, but to contain an absolute treat of a chocolate cake – biscuits, pistachios and luscious buttercream carefully arranged all together inside the glass. Not only is this idea a truly unusual approach, but it is also delightfully delicious.

You will need

- 20cm (8in) round or square chocolate cake, 10cm (4in) high
- 400–500g (14oz–1lb 2oz) chocolate buttercream
- 100–200g (3½–7oz) light green buttercream (Sugarflair Gooseberry)
- 100–200g (3½–7oz) medium green buttercream (Sugarflair Gooseberry)
- Wilton nozzle 150
- Wilton open star nozzle 6B
- Piping bags

- Flower nail
- Baking (parchment) paper
- Scissors
- Digestive biscuits (graham crackers)
- Moss and leaf green edible dust powders
- Re-sealable plastic bag
- Pistachio nuts
- Terrarium glass
- Tray or cake board
- Spoon

1. Pre-pipe and freeze five or six succulent plants in light and medium green buttercream, some 'rose-like' and some 'spiky' (see Piping Flowers).

2. Crumble the biscuits to fine crumbs. Place in a re-sealable bag and add moss and leaf green edible dust powder then shake until you get an even colour.

TIP

You can use a clear glass cake stand with a dome cover as an alternative if you cannot find a terrarium glass ball. Then use a big spoon, fork, tongs or even a small sweet-shop scoop with a pretty ribbon tied around it to serve.

3. Crush some pistachio nuts to make small bits.

4. Cut about a quarter of the cake and break it into pieces, rubbing them together to crumble them into a bowl.

5. Cut the remaining cake into small bite-size squares.

6. Pipe a thin layer of chocolate buttercream on two sides, or all sides, of a cake square, then dip it into the crushed biscuits. Repeat with all the other cake squares.

7. Lay them out on a board, cover with cling film then set them aside. You can cover all the sides of the cake squares with frosting and biscuit if you prefer.

8. Scoop the crumbled cake and biscuit into the terrarium and gently mix together with a spoon.

9. Put the crumbled cake and cake squares into the terrarium, arranging them randomly.

10. Sprinkle in the crushed pistachio nuts. You can also add other types of nuts if you wish. We chose pistachios as they match the moss colour of the crushed biscuits. You can also use small chocolate chips to look like stones or rocks.

11. Finally, put your frozen succulents inside. Arrange them as you wish.

ENCHANTED FOREST FLOWERS

This is our contemporary take on a rustic log cake. It's a million miles from the traditional chocolate Swiss roll! We have created a log with a realistic bark texture, topped with a display of pale and elegant flowers. We think the contrast both enhances and highlights the two elements.

You will need

- 20cm (8in) square cake, 10cm (4in) high
- 400–500g (14oz–1lb 2oz) brown buttercream (Wilton Brown)
- 100–200g (3½–7oz) dark brown buttercream (Sugarflair Dark Brown)
- 100–200g (3½–7oz) white buttercream (Sugarflair Super White powder)
- 100–200g (3½–7oz) dark yellow buttercream (Sugarflair Autumn Leaf)
- 100–200g (3½–7oz) light yellow buttercream (Sugarflair Melon)
- 100–200g (3½–7oz) light purple buttercream (Sugarflair Grape Violet)
- 100–200g (3½–7oz) pale green buttercream (Sugarflair Gooseberry)
- 100–200g (3½–7oz) dark green buttercream (Sugarflair Spruce Green)
- Baking (parchment) paper
- Pencil
- Scissors
- Serrated knife
- Piping bags
- Palette knife
- Small tip palette knife
- Wilton petal nozzle 104
- Wilton leaf nozzle 352
- Wilton chrysanthemum nozzle 81
- Round cookie cutter (optional)

1. Pre-pipe and freeze three white and four light yellow roses using the petal nozzle 104 (see Piping Flowers). Then cut the cake equally in half, and fill and stack the two halves one on top of the other.

2. Cut a circle of baking (parchment) paper with a diameter the same as the width of the cake. Make another identical circle and stick them to both ends of the cake. Then trim off the top with a serrated knife, to make it level with the top of your guide circles.

TIP

You can use the cake trimmings to make cakepops mix by adding a small amount of buttercream to the crumbled cake and mashing it together. This mixture comes in handy to raise up the position of the flowers on the log.

3. Carve the cake into a log shape by following the guide circles. Leave the baking paper on both ends of the cake.

4. Apply the brown buttercream all over the cake except the ends. Use the palette knife to even out the buttercream with short horizontal strokes.

5. Apply blobs of dark brown buttercream and blend with the palette knife using a circular motion. Repeat the same process with a few blobs of dark yellow buttercream.

6. Repeat the short horizontal strokes using the small tip palette knife to create a realistic bark effect.

7. Add small blobs of white buttercream and repeat the same short strokes.

8. Peel off the baking paper circles on the ends of the cake. Apply dark yellow buttercream on both ends, then blend with small blobs of dark brown buttercream using the same palette knife technique.

9. Apply blobs of buttercream on top of the log and position the frozen roses.

10. Pipe the chrysanthemums using the Wilton nozzle 81 in light purple and white with pale geen centres directly onto the cake (see the Charming Chalkboard cake, step 8) to fill in the gaps between the roses.

TIP

11. Pipe the leaves between the flowers with the leaf nozzle 352 using dark green buttercream.

To create the slice of log, use a round cookie cutter or a knife to cut a circle from the excess cake and cover it using the same techniques as described for the log.

VINTAGE BIRD CAGE

Much sought after, vintage bird cages are a favourite amongst collectors of unusual antique items. The shape lends itself perfectly to a domed, single-tier cake, and there are endless possibilities for adding decorative scrolls, flowers or even a bird to create an amazing piece of cake art. Choose elements that compliment the texture and colour of the bird cage to achieve a real masterpiece.

You will need

- 15cm (6in) round cake, 13cm (5in) high
- One 15cm (6in) dome-shaped cake
- Two 15cm (6in) round cake boards
- 20cm (8in) round cake board
- 800–900g (1lb 12oz–2lb) plain buttercream
- 500–600g (1lb 2oz–1lb 5oz) cream buttercream (Sugarflair Cream)
- 200–300g (7–10½oz) chestnut buttercream (Sugarflair Chestnut)
- 200–300g (7–10½oz) lilac buttercream (Sugarflair Lilac)
- 200–300g (7–10½oz) purple buttercream (Sugarflair Grape Violet)
- 200–300g (7–10½oz) peach buttercream (Sugarflair Peach)
- 200–300g (7–10½oz) light green buttercream (Sugarflair Gooseberry)

- Dowels
- Sharpener
- Baking (parchment) paper
- Scissors
- Scraper
- String or thread
- Piping bags
- Wilton small star nozzle 16
- Wilton petal nozzle 103
- Wilton petal nozzle 104
- Wilton leaf nozzle 352
- Pen or pencil
- Glue
- Flower nail

1. Assemble the cake with cake boards in between the second and third layers and one central dowel (see Buttercream Basics). You will need to glue the cake boards together and make a hole in the centre of them before you assemble the stack of cakes so that you can push the central dowel through easily.

2. Crumb coat and cover the cake with a smooth coat of cream buttercream (see Buttercream Basics), then cut a strip of baking (parchment) paper and wrap it around to measure the circumference of the cake.

3. Fold the strip in half again and again until you have as many folds as you want cage bars, and the spaces between look about right, or measure the strip and divide it up. Next cut along two adjacent folds to create a paper guide for the spacing of the cage bars.

4. Use a ruler or scraper to mark a vertical line the full height of the straight side of the cake, then use the paper guide to measure and mark the positions of the bars, around the top and bottom, with a cocktail stick (toothpick). Connect the marks with a ruler or scraper.

5. Cut a strip of parchment paper 2.5cm (1in) in height. Use it to measure and mark the height for the scroll design.

6. To mark the position of the bars on the curved part of the cage, use a piece of string or thread. Align the string to a vertical mark on the side of the cake, then carefully press down the string all the way to the centre of the top. Repeat with all the bars.

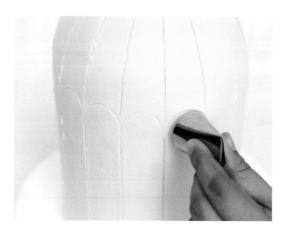

7. Use the opening of a large nozzle or a small round cookie cutter or plunger to mark the curve for the scroll design. Make sure you mark only the upper half of the circle.

8. Use chestnut buttercream in a piping bag with a small hole at the tip to pipe a small shell border (see Piping Textures) for all the bars following your guide marks.

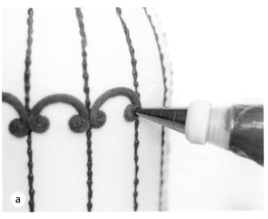 

9. Use the Wilton small star nozzle 16 and chestnut buttercream to pipe the scroll design at the top of the cake sides (a) and loops all around the bottom of the cake (b).

10. Add a conical swirl of chestnut buttercream using the Wilton small star nozzle 16 at the top of the bird cage.

11. Pipe and freeze roses (see Piping Flowers) in assorted sizes using lilac and lavender buttercream. Pipe a blob of cream buttercream and stick the roses on the top and at the base of the cake, then pipe ruffle flowers (see Piping Flowers) using peach buttercream and a Wilton petal nozzle 103, with chestnut centres.

12. Using a piping bag with a small hole at the tip, pipe short wavy green vines down from under the roses. Pipe short spikes alternating on both sides of the vines. Pipe some leaves using the Wilton leaf nozzle 352 in between the flowers.

TIP

When covering a curved surface with buttercream, it's very helpful to have some sort of bendy plastic material handy to help you smooth the surface because you can bend it to match the shape of your desired curve. It could be a thick plastic folder, a mylar or stencil sheet, a plastic placemat, or something similar.

A PAIL OF ROSES

A vintage enamel bucket in the most charming shades of blue, brimming with pastel roses, is so evocative of summer in the garden. This is a simple shape to make with just a little cake carving and allows you to show off your rose piping skills for a special gardening friend's birthday or anniversary.

You will need

- 15 x 10cm (6 x 4in) square cake, 30cm (12in) high
- 10 x 10cm (4 x 4in) round cake or 15cm (6in) dome shaped cake
- 1kg (2lb 4oz) light blue buttercream (Sugarflair Navy Blue)
- 300g (10½oz) dark grey buttercream (Sugarflair Liquorice)
- 100–200g (3½–7oz) light grey buttercream (Sugarflair Liquorice)
- 300g (10½oz) light peach buttercream (Sugarflair Peach)
- 300g (10½oz) medium peach buttercream (Sugarflair Peach)
- 300g (10½oz) light green buttercream (Sugarflair Gooseberry)
- 300g (10½oz) green buttercream (Sugarflair Spruce Green)

- Cake board
- Serrated knife
- Wilton nozzle no.81
- Wilton petal nozzle 104
- Wilton leaf nozzle 352
- Piping bags
- Palette knife
- Cake scraper
- Non-woven cloth
- Baking (parchment) paper
- Scissors
- Pen or pencil
- Bread sticks or thick straight pretzels

1. Before you begin shaping the cake, pipe and freeze 24 roses (you may end up with a few spares) using light and medium peach and light green buttercream (see Piping Flowers). Stack and dowel the cake (see Buttercream Basics) and place it on a cake board but not the final one you will display the cake on. Draw a circle 2.5–5cm (1–2in) smaller than the actual size of your cake on baking (parchment) paper to use as a guide for cutting.

2. Measure 5cm (2in) up from the bottom of the cake, and mark a line all around the cake.

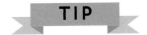

TIP

Because the bottom of the bucket is smaller than the top it is best to start measuring and carving from the smaller end first then just turn the cake upside down.

3. Holding your paper guide circle firmly on the top of the cake, start carving diagonally from the edge of the circle down to the guide line near the bottom.

4. You can also level off around the bottom part of the cake until you get the right 'inverted bucket' shape.

5. Add a thin layer of buttercream on the uppermost surface before putting your final board on top. Insert your hand underneath the lower board, hold both boards firmly, then quickly turn the cake upside down.

6. The wider surface should then be at the top. Place the 10cm (4in) round cake (carved into a small half dome) or a dome-shaped cake on top.

7. Crumb coat the dome cake with untinted buttercream and the rest of the cake in light blue (see Buttercream Basics). Chill in the fridge for about 15–20 minutes or until firm. Add another layer of blue buttercream to the bucket part, then use a scraper to even out the buttercream.

8. Using dark grey buttercream in a piping bag with a small hole cut at the tip, pipe random blobs around the cake. Ensure they are roughly evenly spaced. Then using your palette knife, smear the dark grey buttercream to the blue background using small circular motions.

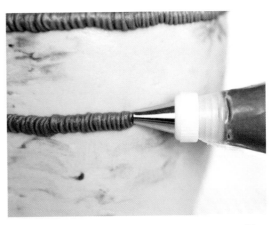

9. Use your cake scraper to even out the surface and to blend the colour better. Scrape in both directions (to the left and to the right) then lightly smooth it with the non-woven cloth (see Buttercream Basics).

10. Add the bucket details using the Wilton nozzle no.81 with the curved part of the nozzle uppermost, and with the nozzle touching the surface. Start at one end and continuously squeeze the piping bag with an even pressure as you move your hand in a tight back and forth movement to give an even texture. Do this at the top edge and the 5cm (2in) mark all the way around the cake.

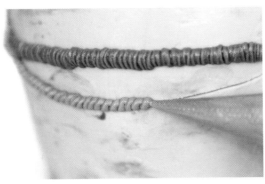

11. Use a cocktail stick (toothpick) to mark where the handle of the bucket should go, then using your light grey buttercream, pipe a loop border following your guide. You can either use the Wilton nozzle no.81 or make a medium-size hole at the tip of your piping bag.

12. Pipe blobs of buttercream at the top to allow you to position the frozen roses at the right angle. Alternate the colours then pipe leaves in between the gaps.

TIP

To make the stem of the roses, cut the breadsticks to your desired length then cover them with Wilton Green Chocolate Candy Melts. Place on baking paper to become firm. (See Autumn Wreath pinecones for instructions on how to pipe roses on breadsticks.)

BOX OF DELIGHTS

Here we have taken what appears to be a shabby package, wrapped in old newspaper, and created a stunning couture ruffles box of deliciously muted colours. Like finding a vintage sewing box or a forgotten parcel of ribbon brooches we hope that the frills, buttons and pearls of this little treasure trove will appeal to you as much as it does to us.

You will need

- 30cm (12in) square cake, 7.5cm (3in) high
- 200–300g (7–10½oz) dusky pink buttercream (Sugarflair Dusky Pink)
- 200–300g (7–10½oz) peach buttercream (Sugarflair Peach)
- 200–300g (7–10½oz) cream buttercream (Sugarflair Caramel)
- 200–300g (7–10½oz) light chestnut buttercream (Sugarflair Chestnut)
- 200–300g (7–10½oz) dark chestnut buttercream (Sugarflair Chestnut)
- 200–300g (7–10½oz) green buttercream (Sugarflair Spruce Green)
- 200–300g (7–10½oz) grey buttercream (Sugarflair Liquorice)
- 200–300g (7–10½oz) light brown buttercream (Sugarflair Dark Brown)
- Printed wafer paper
- Piping gel
- Small bowl
- Paint brush
- Piping bags
- Baking (parchment) paper
- Scissors
- Wilton petal nozzle 104
- Wilton petal nozzle 103
- Wilton nozzle 150
- Wilton nozzle 97L
- Wilton star nozzle 2D

1. Cut the cake in half and stack the two halves one on top of the other. Next crumb coat the cake (see Buttercream Basics).

2. Tear the printed wafer paper sheet into irregular pieces, then position and stick them to the cake. Use piping gel and lightly brush the back of the wafer paper before sticking each piece to the cake.

3. Pipe about 21 guide circles to indicate the position of the ruffles on the top of your cake.

4. Pipe the ruffles onto the cake (see Piping Flowers) with a blob of buttercream beneath, use the photo as a guide.

PASTEL PATCHWORK

Simple squares can create a very contemporary look, particularly when you restrict them to a delicate pastel palette. Keep your squares perfectly square and be accurate with your piping otherwise the effect won't be as good. We've used a different colour combination or texture for each square, mixing the simple and the more intricate. The pale shades enhance the perfection of each square.

You will need

- 20 x 20cm (8 x 8in) square cake, 10cm (4in) high
- 200–300g (7–10½oz) light blue buttercream (Sugarflair Navy Blue)
- 200–300g (7–10½oz) light pink buttercream (Sugarflair Claret)
- 200–300g (7–10½oz) light purple buttercream (Sugarflair Grape Violet)
- 200–300g (7–10½oz) light green buttercream (Sugarflair Gooseberry)
- 200–300g (7–10½oz) light blue-green buttercream (Sugarflair Spruce Green)
- 200–300g (7–10½oz) light peach buttercream (Sugarflair Honey Gold)

- Baking (parchment) paper
- Scissors
- Scraper
- Short angled palette knife
- Small piece of cardboard
- Non-woven cloth
- Wilton chrysanthemum nozzle 81
- Wilton small star nozzle 14
- Wilton plain round nozzle 5
- Wilton basketweave nozzle 47
- Piping bags
- Coupler

1. Stack and crumb coat your cake (see Buttercream Basics). Cut a square of baking (parchment) paper the same size as the top of the cake. Fold it to divide the paper into nine small equal squares.

2. Cut one column of the guide paper and position it on the top of the cake. Use a scraper or ruler to mark out three columns.

TIP

You can use all sorts of other piping techniques to fill the designs for each patch — scrolls, criss-crosses, dots, small piped flowers or anything else you can think of.

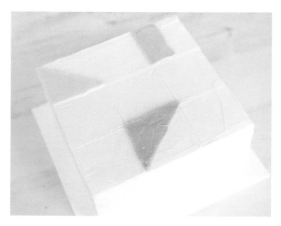

3. Repeat the process to mark the rows. Do the same on the sides of the cake as well.

4. Divide some squares into two, either into rectangles or triangles, using either a scraper or a small piece of cardboard. Apply any choice of tinted buttercream and even it out with the palette knife or the cardboard.

5. Smooth the triangles and rectangles with a non-woven cloth and scraper (see Buttercream Basics).

6. Trim the sides of the shapes in order to make them really straight. Use a scraper, press down and pull it away from the patch. With the edges straight you can repeat steps 4–6 to fill in the other halves of the patches with another colour.

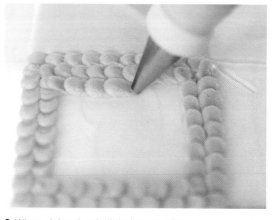

7. If the patch is on the corner edge of the cake, use a scraper and cut downwards. Fill the remaining patches with a variety of colours and textures by swapping the nozzles between different colours of buttercream.

8. When piping the shell design, start from the outer edge using the Wilton plain round nozzle 5. Hold the piping bag at about an 80-degree angle with the opening of the nozzle touching the surface, squeeze until the buttercream builds up then pull the nozzle down.

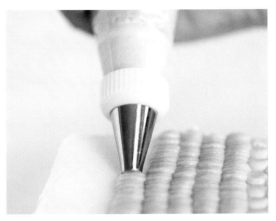

9. When using the chrysanthemum nozzle, make sure the curved part is facing upwards while the two points face down and touch the surface. Start at one end and continuously squeeze the piping bag with an even pressure as you move your hand in a tight back and forth movement to give an even texture.

10. To fill a patch with small stars, start at one end then hold the piping bag at a 90-degree angle with the opening of the nozzle touching the surface, and gently give the bag a good squeeze until it creates a small star. Repeat the same process and make sure you pipe the stars very close together (but not actually overlapping) so that there are no gaps in between.

TIP

This design is very flexible and can be used to create a cake for both men and women. Explore the use of other nozzles and colour combinations to suit your occasion — imagine using gradient colours of pink or blue, it would look amazing! You can also be playful with the shapes. You don't always have to have square patches.

11. To fill a patch using the basketweave nozzle, start at one end choosing either of the sides of the nozzle. Squeeze the piping bag with constant pressure and slowly pull the piping bag down or away. Flip the bag over to pipe alternate stripes of the jagged side of the nozzle and the smooth side.

AZTEC-INSPIRED CHEVRONS

The intricate look of this cake has less to to with the technique of creating it, which is actually really simple, but is based instead on the final effect of the interlocking shapes. We have used a simple small loops piping texture that looks like crochet to make 'V' and inverted 'V' shapes, or chevrons. The result is an impressively distinguished looking pattern.

You will need

- 20cm (8in) round cake, 10cm (4in) high
- 500–600g (1lb 2oz–1lb 5oz) light chestnut buttercream (Sugarflair Chestnut)
- 100–200g (3½–7oz) brown buttercream (Sugarflair Dark Brown)
- 100–200g (3½–7oz) chestnut buttercream (Sugarflair Chestnut)
- 100–200g (3½–7oz) cream buttercream (Sugarflair Cream)
- 100–200g (3½–7oz) blue buttercream (Sugarflair Aztec Blue)

- Baking (parchment) paper
- Ruler
- Pencil
- Scissors
- Small piece of cardboard
- Piping bags
- Scraper or piece of cardboard
- Wafer paper feathers

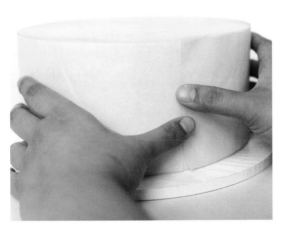

1. Stack, crumb coat and cover the cake in a smooth coat of light chestnut buttercream (see Buttercream Basics). Then cut a strip of baking (parchment) paper that is the exact height and circumference of the covered cake.

2. Keep folding the parchment paper in half until you get sections between the folds of about 1.5cm (⅝in) width.

TIP

This cake design can easily be changed to a different colour scheme to suit your recipient, whether male or female. You can also change the wafer paper appliqué to anything that would suit the design.

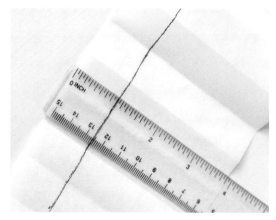

3. Measure 2.5cm (1in) in from one long side and draw a guide line in pencil.

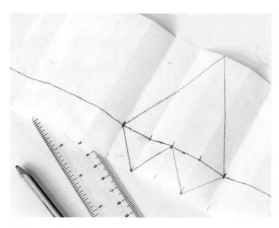

4. Create the chevron shape as shown in the photograph using the folds and the pencil line to guide you.

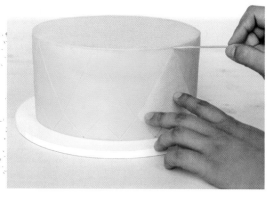

5. Cut out the chevron pattern then place it on the side of the cake with the single point upwards. Use a cocktail stick (toothpick) to mark the outline. Repeat the process to mark chevrons all round the cake side, with each one touching the ones on either side.

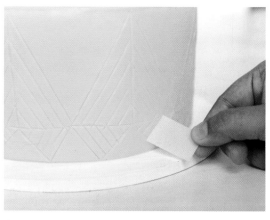

6. Use a small piece of cardboard to mark the centre line and a line across the bottom section of each pattern, then divide the inside of the top part into five strips on each side of the central line. Do this to the bottom part of the chevron as well.

7. Pipe the crochet loops (see 'To pipe the crochet texture') starting from the outermost edge of the pattern. Use brown buttercream for the first rows.

8. Repeat the same process and pipe the crochet texture on the top half of all the chevron patterns using the rest of the colours in the order: chestnut, cream and blue.

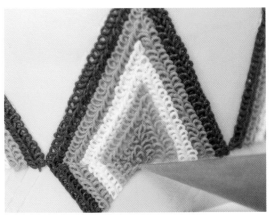

9. Repeat the same process to complete the bottom of the chevrons. Make sure you match the rows with the same colour that you used on the top part of the pattern.

10. Fill in the small triangles left at the base of the chevrons using the same process to pipe the crochet texture. Start the colours again with dark brown, then chestnut and so on.

11. Make the wafer paper feathers by following the instructions in the techniques section. Attach them by applying a small blob of buttercream where you want them to be positioned.

12. Firmly hold the feathers in place for a few seconds to make sure they adhere, before letting go.

To pipe the crochet texture

Pipe two rows of small loops for each colour in the chevron shapes. To pipe the loops, take a piping bag with a small hole at the tip and hold it straight on to the cake with the tip always touching the surface. The first row of loops needs to be counter-clockwise, then the second row is clockwise and slightly overlaps the first row. You can use a Wilton writing nozzle no.1 if you prefer.

BLACK AND WHITE PINSTRIPE

Who wouldn't be drawn to the elegance of a black and white cake? Its simplicity makes it even more dramatic. The vertical pinstripe effect on the sides of the cake has the effect of making it seem taller. To balance this, and at the same time provide a burst of colour, we've added a cascade of button-like flat ruffles, sparkling with lovely edible pearls.

You will need

- 15cm (6in) round cake, 15cm (6in) high
- 1kg (2lb 4oz) white buttercream (Sugarflair Super White powder)
- 100–150g (3½–5½oz) light yellow buttercream (Sugarflair Melon)
- 100–150g (3½–5½oz) medium yellow buttercream (Sugarflair Melon)
- 100–150g (3½–5½oz) grey buttercream (Sugarflair Liquorice)
- 200–300g (7–10½oz) black buttercream (Sugarflair Liquorice)
- Baking (parchment) paper
- Ruler
- Pen or pencil

- Scissors
- Serrated knife
- Short angled palette knife
- Flower nail
- Piping bags
- Scraper
- Wilton nozzle 150
- Wilton basketweave nozzle 47
- Wilton small round nozzle 5
- Large pearl dragees (sugar balls)
- Tweezers

1. Stack and dowel the cake (see Buttercream Basics), then cut a piece of baking (parchment) paper measuring the exact height and circumference of the cake.

2. Fold the paper in half along the side that is the circumference of the cake. On the edge opposite the fold, make a pen mark 2.5cm (1in) from the top, then draw a line from your mark diagonally to the top corner of the folded edge. Trim along the line with scissors.

TIP

When you pipe the stripes it is best that you start from the bottom and pipe upwards. You can use a scraper or ruler to mark straight lines as your guide and just squeeze the piping bag evenly as you quickly pull the bag up to avoid frills.

3. Wrap the baking paper back around the cake and cut with a serrated knife, following your paper guide, to create a sloping top for the cake.

4. Cut small baking paper squares and draw a circle as a size guide. Stick the squares to a flower nail with a blob of buttercream. Hold the Wilton nozzle 150 flat on the surface with the outer edge of the nozzle touching your guide circle. Continuously squeeze the bag as you move your hand in a tight back and forth motion, turning the flower nail and following the guide circle. Repeat to create at least three light yellow, medium yellow and grey ruffles, then freeze them.

5. Crumb coat the cake (see Buttercream Basics). Start piping the stripes on the side of the cake using the Wilton basketweave nozzle 47. Use the jagged edge for white and the smooth side for black. Pipe from the bottom to the top edge of the cake.

TIP

Pipe a couple of spare ruffles so you have some back-ups in case they break when you peel them off the baking paper. They are very delicate as they are made with just a thin layer of buttercream. You also need to work rather quickly when applying them, so that they don't melt before you get the chance to position them. Only press the ruffles in the centre when applying them to the cake so they do not become completely flattened to the surface. They should look three-dimensional.

6. Use the Wilton round nozzle no.5 with white buttercream to cover the top of the cake with a spiral starting from the outer edge and going in. Make sure that there are no gaps in the spiral, and don't lift your piping bag otherwise the buttercream will curl up.

7. Determine where you wish to apply the flat ruffles and then pipe a small blob of buttercream on the cake surface for the first ruffle.

8. Quickly peel off a frozen flat ruffle and position on the cake. Press gently so it adheres properly. Repeat to attach all the ruffles to the cake.

9. Pipe a small blob of buttercream in the centre of each of the flat ruffles and quickly apply a pearl dragee (sugar ball) using tweezers. Press it gently with your finger.

SPARKLING SENSATION

A real show stopper that features edible silver and gold leaf, this cake is proof that even if you feel you lack artistic flair you can still achieve a real work of art with a few palette knife strokes and some sparkle. Use a light hand when blending the colours with your knife and tweezer the metallic leaf into position. You probably won't need anything to make the leaf adhere to the moist surface – buttercream loves gold and silver!

You will need

- 15cm (6in) round cake, 15cm (6in) high
- 500–600g (1lb 2oz–1lb 5oz) white buttercream cake (Sugarflair Super White powder)
- 100–200g (3½–7oz) light blue buttercream (Sugarflair Navy Blue and a hint of Baby Blue)
- 100–200g (3½–7oz) medium blue buttercream (Sugarflair Navy Blue)
- 100–200g (3½–7oz) grey buttercream (Sugarflair Liquorice)
- 100–200g (3½–7oz) green buttercream (Sugarflair Spruce Green)
- 100–200g (3½–7oz) peach buttercream (Sugarflair Peach)
- 50–100g (1¾–3½oz) yellow buttercream (Sugarflair Autumn Leaf)
- Piping bags
- Scissors
- Scraper
- Short angled palette knife
- Small bowl of water
- Tweezers
- Edible gold and silver leaves
- Wilton petal nozzle 104
- Wilton petal nozzle 103

1. Stack and crumb coat your cake, then apply a coat of white buttercream (see Buttercream Basics). Even out the buttercream on the sides with a scraper after applying it. The surface doesn't need to be perfectly smooth.

2. For the top of the cake, after applying the buttercream, even it out with a scraper and use the tip of your palette knife to make a spiral texture starting from the edge of the cake and moving towards the centre.

3. Use a cocktail stick (toothpick) to make a guide mark as to where you will apply your gold and silver leaves.

4. Pipe small blobs of light blue buttercream all around the bottom part of the cake. Make the blobs random but roughly evenly spaced. Keep below the line you have marked by about 5cm (2in).

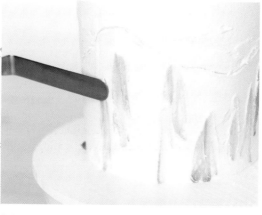

5. Spread the buttercream with the tip of your palette knife using upward strokes. Avoid going back and forth too much.

6. Repeat the same process with medium blue and grey buttercream, but use less grey than the blues.

7. Add just a few hints of both blues and the grey above the line. Do not overdo it. If the buttercream is starting to crust and it becomes hard to spread the colours, dip the tip of your palette knife into a little water. Make sure that you do not put too much water on your cake though.

8. Using your tweezers, peel a small piece of gold leaf and apply it to the cake following your guide mark.

9. Repeat the process to build up the gold and silver leaves to cover your guide mark. Use more gold leaves than silver. You can also apply some metallic flecks randomly on the sides of the cake.

10. Pipe three leaves in green, radiating out from the point where a flower will be, using the Wilton petal nozzle 104 and a two-stroke piping technique (see Piping Flowers). Pipe three more leaves for the second flower.

TIP

When applying the gold and silver leaves, make sure you use tweezers. The metallic leaf is very delicate and will easily rip in your fingers. Since fresh buttercream already has a sticky surface, the leaf easily adheres to it. If the buttercream has crusted too much though, you can brush the surface with water or a very thin application of piping gel.

11. Pipe a blob of buttercream in the centre of each cluster of leaves to give the flower a nice volume. Pipe a ruffle flower (see Piping Flowers) on top of each blob using the Wilton petal nozzle 103 with peach buttercream. Add yellow dots to the flowers' centres using a piping bag with a small hole at the tip.

ALL GOLD

An opulent glow created with just the right combination of bronze and gold, makes this cake a gorgeous gift for someone who appreciates the finer things in life. It is simplicity itself to create but makes a sublime statement, almost appearing to shine on its own.

You will need

- 20cm (8in) square cake, 10cm (4in)
- 700–800g (1lb 9oz–1lb 12oz) untinted buttercream
- 200–300g (7–10½in) dark yellow buttercream (Sugarflair Autumn Leaf)
- Baking (parchment) paper
- Small piece of cardboard or stiff paper
- Ruler
- Pen or pencil
- Serrated knife
- Scissors
- Scraper
- Palette knife

- Piping bags
- Cocktail stick (toothpick)
- Airbrush machine
- Dinky Doodle gold airbrush paint
- Edible gold leaves
- Piping gel
- Paint brush
- Small bowls
- Rainbow Dust gold and bronze edible paint
- Gold sugar sprinkles (nonpareils)
- Wafer paper

1. In advance, pre-pipe around 30 to 35 small roses (see Piping Flowers) using untinted buttercream, and freeze them. If you want the roses to look lighter, you can tint the buttercream white using Sugarflair Super White powder.

2. Carve your cake referring to the Toile de Jouy cake for instructions on how to prepare the octagonal shape. Crumb coat, then cover the cake with a smooth coat of plain buttercream (see Buttercream Basics). Use the cocktail stick (toothpick) to divide the cake into sections, making the lines slightly wavy rather than straight.

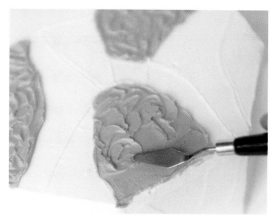

3. Choose the sections where you want the textured airbrushing to go. Begin with these by applying a thin layer of dark yellow buttercream. Use the tip of a narrow round-tip palette knife and sweep in a round motion in both clockwise and counter-clockwise directions.

4. Use edible gold airbrush paint and spray over the textured section until it is evenly coated. Do not bring the spray gun too close to the surface or the colours may pool or drip.

5. Choose the sections you want to cover with edible gold leaf. If the surface of the cake is still fresh, the gold leaf will easily adhere to the surface. If not, brush the surface with a thin layer of piping gel. Cut the gold leaf according to each section's shape then pull back one side of the backing paper and stick the gold leaf to the surface.

6. As the gold leaf sticks to the surface, gently slide your hand away and pull the rest of the backing paper out. You can use the backing paper to rub the gold leaf gently to help it to stick more, instead of using your fingers as it will easily stick to them.

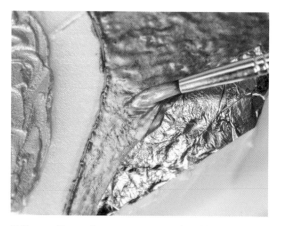

7. Choose the sections you want to paint with metallic colours. Use the edible bronze paint to apply the first layer of colour. Let it dry slightly for about 10 to 15 minutes then paint over with edible gold paint and lightly blend the two colours together.

8. The remaining sections will be filled with gold sugar sprinkles (non-pareils). Apply a thin layer of piping gel on the surface using a paint brush.

9. Use your fingers to sprinkle the gold sugar sprinkles on the sections you need to fill. You can also use a cocktail stick or a dry paint brush to spread out the tiny balls.

10 Prepare the gold wafer paper leaves by painting both sides with bronze paint first then smear it with gold (see the techniques section for information on using wafer paper). Let it dry completely.

11. Cut small leaf shapes from the dried gold wafer paper using a pair of scissors.

12. Place the frozen roses all around the bottom of the cake. Pipe small blobs of buttercream behind each one so it sticks and is slightly angled.

13. Insert the cut-out wafer paper leaves in between the roses.

PINK SHIMMER

There will always be something glamorous about shimmering metallic cakes. The cascade of sparkling sugar crystals on this eye-catching creation brings a touch of sophistication, offering something decadent and yet remaining simple and modern.

You will need

- 20cm (8in) round cake, 15cm (6in) high
- 1kg (2lb 4oz) white buttercream (Sugarflair Super White powder)
- 100–200g (3½–10½oz) black buttercream (Sugarflair Liquorice)
- Airbrush machine
- Dinky Doodle pearl and silver airbrush paint (oil-based)
- 450–500g (1lb–1lb 2oz) jam making/preserving sugar (very big granules), or use granulated if you can't find preserving sugar.
- Rainbow Dust pink and silver edible metallic paint
- Re-sealable bags

- Baking (parchment) paper
- Palette knife
- Tray or pizza pan
- Paint brush
- Piping gel
- Scraper or piece of cardboard
- Wafer paper
- Sugarflair Liquorice food colouring paste
- Florist wire gauge 27 (or anything thin)
- Piping bags
- Scissors
- Small bowls

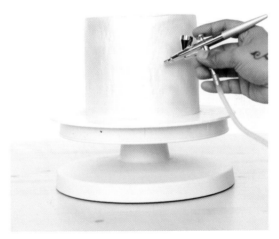

1. Refer to the techniques section for instructions on how to assemble the wafer paper flower. Airbrush the tip of each of the petals with silver airbrush paint. You can make this flower ahead of time (see Tip).

2. Stack and crumb coat, then cover the cake with a smooth coat of white buttercream (see Buttercream Basics). When it is crusted enough, airbrush with pearl airbrush paint.

TIP

Prepare the wafer paper petals for the black flower individually in small, medium and large sizes, then put them together to create the flower. You can airbrush the petals with pearl paint to match the cake if you wish.

3. Prepare the coloured sugar sprinkles by putting 150g (5½oz) of preserving sugar in a re-sealable bag and then adding drops of pink edible metallic paint to it.

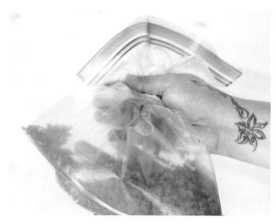

4. Shake the bag until the colour is evenly distributed. You can add more colour to make it darker but be careful not to use too much as it can start to dissolve the sugar. Repeat the same process to create a total of three different shades of pink.

5. Spread the sugar out on a piece of baking (parchment) paper to allow it to dry, using a palette knife. Leave it to air dry overnight, or bake at 180°C or 350°F for ten minutes.

6. When dried, the colour will be lighter and it will look like chunks of sugar crystals. You can put the sugar into a re-sealable bag once more and gently crush it to separate the crystals.

7. Place the cake on to a tray or a pizza pan then brush the bottom part of the cake with piping gel. Brush it all around the cake covering the area where you want the darker sugar crystals to be. Note that you will be flipping the cake over later, so the bottom will become the top.

8. Sprinkle the darkest pink sugar crystals all around the base and lightly press them on the cake, covering everywhere that the piping gel was brushed.

9. Repeat the same process creating layers above with the remaining two shades of pink. When applying the sugar crystals to the cake, it is easier to use a piece of cardboard or scraper to apply these upper layers.

10. Give the last layer of sugar crystals a ragged uneven edge, to add drama to the design.

11. Pipe a thin layer of buttercream on top of the cake then place a cake board over it. Hold the tray (or pizza pan) and the cake board firmly then quickly but carefully flip the cake over.

12. Apply a thin layer of black buttercream on top, let it crust, then smooth it.

13. Sprinkle the darkest shade of sugar crystals (the first one you used on the cake side) all around the top edge of the cake, then lightly press the crystals so they adhere to the cake properly.

14. Lightly airbrush with edible pearl paint all around the cake to give it even more sparkle and to cover up some of the gaps between the sugar crystals. Finish by adding the wafer paper flower.

STEAMPUNK HAT

Steampunk is all about mixing the style of the Victorian age with modern technological accessories. It commonly features lots of brass, bronze or copper, and is very often accessorized with fashion features including corsetry, feathers and brooches. Applying this theme to a cake means infusing all the details with quirky style and elegance.

You will need

- 15cm (6in) round cake, 15cm (6in) high
- 20cm (8in) round x 2.5cm (1in) thick styrofoam cake dummy
- 800–900g (1lb 12oz–2lb) black buttercream (Sugarflair Liquorice)
- 400–500g (14oz–1lb 2oz) brown buttercream (Sugarflair Dark Brown)
- 30–50g (1¼–1¾oz) light brown buttercream (Wilton Brown)
- 300–400g (10½–14oz) dark violet buttercream (Sugarflair Grape Violet)
- 300–400g (10½–14oz) violet buttercream (Sugarflair Grape Violet plus Claret)
- 50–100g (1¾–3½oz) yellow buttercream (Sugarflair Autumn Leaf)
- Dowels
- Scissors
- Baking (parchment) paper
- Ruler
- Pencil
- Piping bags
- Scraper
- Impression mat
- Airbrush machine
- Non-woven cloth
- Dinky Doodle gold airbrush paint
- Wilton petal nozzle 103
- Wilton petal nozzle 104
- Brooch moulds
- Small piece of card for marking
- Gold dragees (sugar balls)
- Tweezers
- Wafer paper feather

1. Stack then carve the cake (see Buttercream Basics). For guidance on how to achieve the correct shape refer to the Pail of Roses cake. When you are happy with the shape, flip the cake over and crumb coat it (see Buttercream Basics).

2. Cut a strip of baking (parchment) paper about 2.5cm (1in) wide and the exact circumference of the cake, then position it 2.5cm (1in) down from the top edge of the cake. From a square of baking paper 2.5cm (1in) shorter than the height of your cake, cut a big 'V' shape of whatever size you want the laced part of the design to be. Cut it in two halves vertically and stick it to the freshly crumbcoated cake, then trim the baking paper strip to open up the top of the V, as shown. Cover the cake top and inside of the V, as well as the styrofoam cake dummy, with black buttercream.

3. Let the black buttercream areas dry and crust at room temperature for a good 45 minutes to an hour, or until they are not sticky to the touch. Then lightly press all the black buttercream with your impression mat. Cover the cake dummy for the hat brim in the same way.

4. Lightly airbrush with gold, making sure that the spray gun is not too close to the cake so the colour does not pool on the surface or form drips. Do the same on the styrofoam cake dummy.

5. Gently peel the baking paper off. You can use a cocktail stick (toothpick) to help you carefully lift the paper up.

6. Cover the sides of the cake with brown buttercream. Even it up with a scraper or palette knife then smooth with a non-woven cloth (see Buttercream Basics).

7. Pipe some random scrolls on all the sides using the same brown buttercream in a piping bag with a small hole at the tip. Alternatively, you could use a Wilton writing nozzle no.1 if you prefer.

8. Next assemble the parts. Place the covered styrofoam cake dummy onto your cake board then stack the cake on top of it, centrally. Cut a piece of dowel that is the total height of the cake then insert it in the centre (see Buttercream Basics).

9. Use the petal nozzle 103 and dark violet buttercream to pipe the ruffles border (see Piping Textures) all around the top of the brown area, and along the edge of the V shape. Always make sure that the wider part of the nozzle is at the bottom. If you wish you can pipe two or three layers of ruffles – we stopped at one.

10. Pipe two or three layers of non-wavy ruffles in dark violet where the hat crown meets the brim.

11. Pipe some ruffle flowers (see Piping Flowers) in a variety of sizes and position your frozen rose or roses (see tip). Then add the gold-airbrushed frozen brooch moulds in the centre of each ruffle flower.

12. Make criss-cross marks on the black V-shaped area using a small piece of card, then pipe over the marks using the loop border technique (see Piping Textures) using light brown buttercream. Place edible gold balls on the point where the 'laces' meet the edging ruffles.

TIP

Pre-pipe one or two roses using violet buttercream, and fill brooch moulds with yellow buttercream then freeze them in advance (see Piping Flowers). Airbrush the brooches with gold when done.

13. Add the wafer paper feather to finish (see the techniques section for instructions on using wafer paper). If you prefer, you can position this before you add the rose and ruffles.

NICELY SLICED

Why stick with one motif for a whole cake? Here you can experiment with half a dozen
complementary designs! However you slice it, this cake creates a visual feast.
Even if you go for the simplest of patterns, this is still a show-stopping
way to present a cake and is bound to impress.

You will need

- 200–250g (7–9oz) of each of the following colours of buttercream: deep pink (Sugarflair Claret), blue (Sugarflair Baby Blue plus a hint of Navy), purple (Sugarflair Grape Violet), yellow (Sugarflair Melon with a hint of Autumn Leaf), orange (Sugarflair Orange), green (Sugarflair Spruce Green)
- 100–150g (3½–5½oz) white buttercream (Sugarflair Super White powder)
- 50g (1¾oz) red buttercream (Sugarflair Ruby Red)
- 20cm (8in) round cake, 10cm (4in) high
- Scraper
- Non-woven cloth

- Wilton nozzle 102
- Wilton petal nozzle 103
- Wilton leaf nozzle 352
- Wilton star nozzle 14
- Wilton ruffle nozzle 86
- Piping bags
- Baking (parchment) paper
- Pencil or pen
- Scissors
- Serrated knife
- Button moulds
- Pearl dragees (sugar balls)

1. Cut out a circle of baking (parchment) paper that is the same size at the top of your cake.

2. Fold the paper in half, then fold twice more to make three equally sized triangles.

TIP

We chose fun and bright colours for our theme, but why not see what effect you can achieve with pastel shades or maybe a monochromatic scheme? Imagination is the only limitation!

3. Use a serrated knife to remove the top of the cake to create a flat surface. Unfold the pattern to a half circle then place it over the cake, and follow the pattern to slice the cake.

4. Fold to a triangle again then repeat the same process. Crumb coat and cover the slices with a smooth coat of your chosen colour of buttercream (see Buttercream Basics). Then decorate as you wish, or by following one of our designs.

Blue flowery slice

Mark a guide halfway up the sides of the slice and pipe ruffles all around using Wilton nozzle 86 (see Piping Textures). Use white buttercream and Wilton nozzle 14 to pipe small flowers all over the upper part of the cake. Top them with pink dragees (sugar balls). Pipe a small ruffle flower on top (see Piping Flowers) and put a moulded buttercream button (see Moulds) in the centre, and finish off with some small leaves. Pipe the top border using Wilton nozzle 14 in a tight zigzag motion.

Pink slice

Pipe downward ruffles (see Piping Textures) starting from the top edge of the cake using Wilton petal nozzle 103 in two-tone pink (see Lace Romance cake). Use Wilton leaf nozzle 352 to pipe long leaves. Pipe small five- or six-petalled flowers on top using Wilton petal nozzle 102 and finish off with pearl dragees on the centres.

Purple slice

Pipe a wavy border around the sides of the cake using Wilton basketweave nozzle 47 with the smooth side up, then pipe a shell border (see Piping Textures) all around the top edge of the cake. You can add blue dragees on each corner for a little variation. Pipe some scrolls on the top surface and a simple petal flower (see Piping Flowers) using Wilton petal nozzle 102 and finish off with a moulded buttercream button (see Moulds).

Blue ribboned slice

Pipe some scrolls on the sides of the cake using just a piping bag with a small hole at the tip, or writing nozzle no.2. Pipe some small random ruffle flowers (see Piping Flowers) directly on the side of the cake adding pearl dragees to the centres. The top and bottom edges of the slice are decorated with a shell border (see Piping Textures). On the top surface, use Wilton petal nozzle 102 and pipe a ruffled ribbon and finish with some pink dragees in the centre.

Orange slice

Pipe back to back ruffles (see Piping Textures) on the side of the cake with a shell border where the ruffles meet, as well as along the top edge of the cake. Pipe a single layer of ruffle using Wilton petal nozzle 102 at the top of the cake following the shape of the curve and finish off with colourful moulded buttercream buttons (see Moulds). Pipe a bead border at the bottom edge.

Yellow slice

Pipe some random swirls on the side of the cake using yellow buttercream. Add back to back ruffles (see Piping Textures) topped with pearl dragees in a curve to echo the shape of the slice. Use pink and red buttercream in a piping bag with a small hole at the tip and pipe two 'C's facing each other to create the small flower effect, and add short wavy lines for the leaves. Pipe a contrasting shell border at the base and finish with dragees at the corners.

137

ALICE IN WONDERLAND

This is a really eccentric cake – it reflects our very active imaginations! We wanted
to create a fun design that plays with colours in an appealing and cheerful
way. The result is a cake fantasy that is actually produced using some
pretty simple techniques. And what could be more whimsical
than a Mad Hatter's tea party theme?

You will need

- Two 15cm (6in) half dome cakes
- 30cm (12in) round cake board
- 400–500g (14oz–1lb 2oz) plain buttercream
- 500–600g (1lb 2oz–1lb 5oz) light pink buttercream (Sugarflair Claret)
- 200–300g (7–10½oz) dark yellow buttercream (Sugarflair Autumn Leaf)
- 100–200g (3½–7oz) light yellow buttercream (Sugarflair Honey Gold)
- 100–200g (3½–7oz) blue buttercream (Sugarflair Baby Blue plus Navy Blue)
- 300–400g (10½–14oz) yellow buttercream (Sugarflair Melon)
- 300–400g (10½–14oz) violet buttercream (Sugarflair Grape Violet)
- 300–400g (10½–14oz) red buttercream (Sugarflair Red Extra)
- 300–400g (10½–14oz) dark green buttercream (Sugarflair Spruce Green)
- 100–200g (3½–7oz) light green buttercream (Sugarflair Gooseberry)
- 100–150g (3½–5½oz) dark pink buttercream (Sugarflair Scarlet)
- Flower nail
- Baking (parchment) paper
- Scissors
- Serrated knife
- 15cm (6in) round, 2.5cm (1in) thick styrofoam board
- Small palette knife
- Piping bags
- Wilton round nozzle no.10
- Wilton writing nozzle no.5
- Wilton petal nozzle 103
- Wilton leaf nozzle 352
- Wilton open star nozzle 1M
- Wilton Candy Melts, pink
- Small bowl for melting
- Cocktail stick (toothpick)
- Chocolate-covered pretzel
- Pink chocolate button

1. Pre-pipe and freeze around 20 roses in red, violet and yellow buttercream (see Piping Flowers). Join the two half dome cakes to make a sphere. Using the serrated knife, trim off the rounded top, then make a downward cut from the top centre about 2.5cm (1in) deep, and another horizontal cut from the side to take out a segment as shown.

2. Flip the cake over and sit it on the clock as shown, with the part with the missing segment resting on the clock.

3. Trim off the rounded top of the cake to make it flat, then crumb coat (see Buttercream Basics). Cover the cake with a smooth coat of light pink buttercream. Using a large cake board (about 30cm/12in diameter) secure the cake firmly with a good amount of buttercream, or you may use a dowel (see Buttercream Basics) that goes through the cake board for added support.

4. Pipe ruffles all around the flat top part of the teapot using light yellow buttercream and petal nozzle 103. Fill the centre as you pipe each layer of ruffles to make it into a slight dome.

5. Stack three or four pink buttons, created and frozen using a mould (see Moulds) on top of the ruffles in the centre, to look like the knob of the teapot lid.

6. Pipe some scrolls for stems onto the side of the teapot using light green buttercream in a piping bag with a small hole at the tip.

To make the clock

For the clock you can use a real cake, but we used a 15cm (6in) round, 2.5cm (1in) thick styrofoam board. Just trim the top edge of the board to make it slightly rounded. Cover the top with plain buttercream and blend in some dark yellow buttercream with a palette knife then smooth the surface (see the sky instructions in the Country Window cake). Next, cover the side with dark yellow buttercream then pipe a simple border around the top with the round nozzle no.10, then a narrower one inside that with the writing nozzle no. 5. Finally, pipe the hands and Roman numerals on the clockface using black buttercream in a piping bag with a small hole at the tip.

7. Pipe small buds in blue buttercream using the petal nozzle 103 (see Piping Flowers) and even smaller buds with just a piping bag with a small hole at the tip. Pipe some spikes with fat bases and tapering points on the side of the stems for leaves using light green buttercream and a piping bag with a medium hole at the tip.

8. Position the roses around the cake, as shown, using cocktail sticks (toothpicks) to manoeuvre them if necessary. Secure them with blobs of buttercream.

9. Pipe the leaves in between the flowers using dark green buttercream and the leaf nozzle 352.

10. Use the open star nozzle 1M and dark pink buttercream to pipe the base where you will attach the handle of the teapot. Hold the nozzle straight on to the cake and firmly squeeze the piping bag to build up a big star.

11. Melt the pink Candy Melts and cover a couple of pretzels. Allow them to cool, then attach them on the star you piped for the handle. Or you can create a handle using wafer paper (see Using Wafer Paper in the techniques section).

12. Pipe the spout by positioning the nozzle a little below the midline of the cake then squeezing the piping bag with slow steady pressure until you reach the desired length of the spout. Slowly pull away as you continue to squeeze. Stick a pink moulded button at the tip.

Suppliers

UK SUPPLIERS

Queen of Hearts Couture Cakes
23 Jersey Road, Hanwell,
London, W7 2JF
+44 (0)1634 235407 / 075813 95801
www.queenofheartscouturecakes.com
Supplier of food colouring pastes and
cake decorating materials

Wilton UK
Merlin Park, Wood Lane, Erdington
Birmingham B24 9Ql
0121 386 3200
www.wilton.co.uk
Big selection of nozzles and cake
decorating supplies

DinkyDoodle Designs
2b Triumph Road,
Nottingham, NG7 2GA
+44 (0)115 969 9803
www.dinkydoodledesigns.co.uk
Supplier of airbrush machines
and colours

US SUPPLIER

The Wilton Store
7511 Lemont Road
Darien, IL 60561
+1 (630) 985 6000
www.wilton.com
Big selection of nozzles and
cake decorating supplies

About the authors

Queen of Hearts Couture Cakes is a multi-award winning cake company based in London, UK. This company, which has gone from strength to strength since its beginning in 2011, is owned and run by best friends, Valeri Valeriano and Christina Ong. They have authored two best-selling books, *The Contemporary Buttercream Bible* and *100 Buttercream Flowers* which were released 2014 and 2015 respectively. Valeri and Christina have discovered that they can create stunning edible works of art using nothing else but buttercream and since then, they have never looked back.

These self-taught ladies offer the most intensive and extensive number of buttercream techniques through classes in Europe, USA, Asia, Middle East and Australia. They have been featured in well known magazines, local and international news and have appeared in various TV shows. They have been highlighted as international cake stars in different renowned cake shows internationally as they showcase their masterpieces.

Queen of Hearts Couture Cakes creations always deliver originality, sophistication, elegance and perfection.

Thanks

"Choose a job you love, and you will never have to work a day in your life." Confucius

Our cake journey has been the best years of our lives so far. We have always believed that there must be one great purpose for why things turn out as they do. To those who believed in us, supported us, inspired us and were inspired by us, thank you for being a part of our journey.

To our F+W Media family: Ame Verso, Lorraine Inglis and Anna Wade, thank you for always trusting us, so that together we could make a little bit of cake decorating history. To Sam Vallance for helping us spread buttercream love in different languages.

To our fairy cake editor, Jane Trollope, we can't thank you enough. Jason Jenkins, your passion for making sure that we got the best photos is amazing, thank you for always going for that 'last shot' (even when we'd asked for it ten times already).

To Justine Hyde of Hyde+Seek, Exeter for letting us borrow some of her gorgeous stock for our photoshoot.

To our Cake International family, Clare Fisher, Ben Fidler, Troy Bennett, Melanie Underwood, Adam Elkins, Vicky Vinton, David Bennett, Simon Burns and to everyone else, thank you for always believing in us. We will be forever grateful and proud to be a part of your family and your shows every year.

To our new friends at Wilton, thank you for welcoming us and supporting us always in all ways.

To our increasing number of loyal friends around the world, thank you for being buttercream believers, you are all superstars.

To our families back in the Philippines, we love you. Our success story is your story. Thank you for being proud of us. This is for you.

Go #TEAMBUTTERCREAM!

Index

A DAVID & CHARLES BOOK
© F&W Media International, Ltd 2016

David & Charles is an imprint of F&W Media International, Ltd
Brunel House, Forde Close, Newton Abbot, TQ12 4PU, UK

F&W Media International, Ltd is a subsidiary of F+W Media, Inc
10151 Carver Road, Suite #200, Blue Ash, OH 45242, USA

Text and Designs © Valeri Valeriano and Christina Ong 2015
Layout and Photography © F&W Media International, Ltd 2016
First published in the UK and USA in 2016

ISBN-13: 978-1-4463-0621-5 paperback
ISBN-10: 1-4463-0621-6 paperback

ISBN-13: 978-1-4463-7340-8 PDF
ISBN-10: 1-4463-7340-1 PDF

ISBN-13: 978-1-4463-7339-2 EPUB
ISBN-10: 1-4463-7339-8 EPUB

Printed in USA by RR Donnelley for:
F&W Media International, Ltd
Brunel House, Forde Close, Newton Abbot, TQ12 4PU, UK

10 9 8 7 6 5 4 3 2

Acquisitions Editor: Ame Verso
Desk Editor: Michelle Patten
Project Editor: Jane Trollope
Designer / Stylist: Lorraine Inglis
Art Editor: Anna Wade
Photographer: Jason Jenkins
Production Controller: Bev Richardson

F+W Media publishes high quality books on a wide range of subjects.
For more great book ideas visit: www.stitchcraftcreate.co.uk

Layout of the digital edition of this book may vary depending on reader hardware and display settings.